MW00937235

BLACK WOMEN DESERVE BETTER

CW

Outskirts Press, Inc.
Denver, Colorado

Black Women Deserve Better
All Rights Reserved.
Copyright © 2008 CW
V1.0

Outskirts Press, Inc.
http://www.outskirtspress.com

ISBN: 978-1-4327-2103-9

Outskirts Press and the "OP" logo are trademarks belonging to Outskirts Press, Inc.

PRINTED IN THE UNITED STATES OF AMERICA

The Book That Will Turn the Black Community on its Head!

For Black women (and their admirers) who wish to expand their dating options...

Dare to step outside of the box!

"Black Women Deserve Better" Dares To Ask…

-Are Black women often pressured to stick it out with just any Black man?

-Fool me once: How Black women get fooled again.

-Are Black women simply imagining how dire the situation has become?

-Identifying the fallacy concerning a "forever happily single" mantra.

-Has the Black community double crossed Black women?

ABOUT THE AUTHOR

CW is a 31-year-old woman native to Brooklyn, NY. She currently resides the Hampton Roads area of Virginia. CW has worked as a police/EMS dispatcher for the past six years. She began expanding her dating options a little over a year ago to include men of all races. CW's blog, "Black Women Deserve Better," was an exercise in self-discovery and healing. She is an only child who lives with her illustrious orange tabby cat, Deveraux. CW is an avid "I Love Lucy" fan who enjoys reading, movies, seminars, car shows, flea markets, dancing, and discussing politics. CW's mission is to help Black women get the love, respect, and commitment they deserve.

INTRODUCTION

Black men are continually being taught to disrespect, dishonor, and disregard the Black woman. The ugly, heartbreaking results manifest themselves with the "baby mama" epidemic, video vixen mentality, enabling, denial, and other self-defeating behaviors. Yes, the Black man has a lot of work to do; however, Black woman can only control her own responses and actions.

"Black Women Deserve Better" reveals the mind control and deceptions used by our own people to keep Sisters in their place. Resolve not only to want change, but also to *be the change*. Our daughters are counting on us!

This book is dedicated to every Black woman who:

- Has tirelessly searched for answers from those who will not tell her the truth

- Wants better for her daughter

- Is afraid to bring up the subject for fear of ridicule

- Has done all the "right" things and yet wonders how everything could go so wrong

- Has witnessed the state of Black man/woman relations decline since her youth

CONTENTS

Commonly Used Abbreviations:

CW: Author
BW/BF: Black woman/female
BM: Black man
WM: White man
WW/WF: White woman/female

WHO IS CW?

My name is Cherilyn Weekes, aka CW. I hail from Brooklyn, NY, and currently reside in the Hampton Roads area of Virginia. I moderate a blog called "Black Women Deserve Better." Bottom line, because we do. "Black Women Deserve Better" and forums like it are way overdue. There have been several catalysts which have prompted me to write this book. My desire is to bring Black women hope and clarity in a very troubling time for our families. During my short thirty-one years on this planet, I have witnessed and experienced the rapid deterioration of Black man/Black woman relationships. It is disheartening to see Black women from all walks of life go though an earthly hell. From the college educated and entrepreneur, to the single mother or the young woman coming into her own, we all share one common denominator: Interpersonal relationships with Black men are the pits! There, I said it aloud!

But before the stones are hurled in my direction please finish reading and take time to digest the content. My words are going to be contrary to the rhetoric that has been programmed into women's minds since infancy.

This writing will not inundate the reader with endless statistics which do not help to solve the problem. I want the Black woman to think independently, to begin relying on her instincts. Black women cannot remain in the same mindset from years gone by. We cannot expect change by holding on to the same beliefs, going through the same motions. Our goals may be similar or completely different from one another. One truth remains consistent: We need to start putting ourselves in motion. Tune out the noise, and closely observe the actions of Black males in the environment. Put aside all of the fist-in-the-air Black Power slogans of yesterday. Are Black women alone? Only when we are not needed to toe the line for a variety of civil rights causes.

Since starting the Black Women Deserve Better Web site, I have received plenty of feedback from both men and women. Varying points of view are presented in this writing. Black women have had these discussions amongst themselves for year. Sisters, we are not alone. Please do not operate in a place of false pride and shame like I did for so long. For years I blamed myself for not being able to find a quality Black man. Up until recently, I believed God had abandoned me. My summation was that I was unworthy of love. I was too deeply ashamed to admit this to anyone. My response was an attempt to make myself as attractive as possible, inside and out, to avoid rejection. I read scores of books, attended seminars, and took notes from all the self-help gurus. Armed with all of this knowledge, I was a shoe-in for the best love life possible. Or so I thought. I was getting ready and "perfect" for that mate while simultaneously hiding the same desire as not to appear desperate. The years passed and nothing changed but the weather. The blinders had to be painfully ripped from my eyes. Right now, Black women need to get their lives into gear. Sisters have been scammed into accepting a raw deal and not seeing our situation for what it truly is. Downhill was about ten years ago. This is a full-blown red-alarm emergency. Would anyone care to imagine what our little Black girls would have to look forward to in fifteen to twenty years? I shudder to think.

A Very Revealing Year in Dating

To say my romantic experiences over the last decade have been disappointing would be an understatement. I will spare the reader and shorten the time frame to one year. Here is the story of a dozen men that I have dated within that timeframe. Four of the men were Black, the remainder were of different races. Since consciously deciding to give men of all races a chance, dating has become fun again.

Critical thinking for Black women who are not open to interracial dating:

- When was the last time you went out on a proper date?
- Are you raising your Black child alone?

I am sad to report that my experience in dating men of other races were polar opposites from the Black men. Even when things did not progress into a relationship, I had a wonderful time and was treated like a lady. These men made no attempts to tear me down. Things were pretty straightforward. It was night and day. What I have observed is the scam being run by many Black men in the dating world. At the risk of generalizing, I have found this disingenuous behavior to be found predominantly with Black men. One would think that I were only describing the antics of young men in their teens to early twenties. Age did not greatly affect the utilization of the scam. Keep in mind when someone runs a scam, they are using deception to take what belongs to the victim. The scam artist has no intentions of reciprocity. He wants to obtain something with value without working for it. Sistas, do not get scammed into giving sex, material resources, or time without prerequisites.

The first Black man I've dated this year (thirty-six years old) told me on our second date that he did not want anything serious. He proclaimed that he wanted to "take things slow." That was fine with me. I was being introduced to and dating other men. Don't get me wrong; I'd love to be married and have a baby. Just not nine months from today! Well, lo and behold the phone rings less than a week later. This man is now whining about how I don't call. No, I am just not going to buy into the scam: giving the disclaimer that a relationship is not desired while simultaneously trying to get all of the benefits thereof. Then when this man is done with the scam he can say with a clear conscience, "I told you that I didn't want anything serious." Being in the closing room with a used-car salesman is more pleasurable than this charade.

The second Black man I dated was in his early twenties. In retrospect, I could see he had the "How To Be The Ultimate Supreme Playa-Playa" handbook well memorized. We went out on three dates. On the second, we kissed (shows interest, I think). On the third date, this guy was constantly answering his cell phone during the date. Where is the home training? That revealed a lot to me and I should have made it the last date. In an attempt to be flexible, I temporarily looked past this faux pas. Anyway, this brother applied a page out of the handbook called "I Pretend Not To Like You This Week, So That I Can Get What I Want Next Week." I didn't buy *the scam* and asked the brother after about two months what was going on. Briefly digressing, another bill of goods (especially geared towards Black women) is that we are not supposed to ask questions about his intentions. This is one of the doctrines that we have to deprogram ourselves from. My interpersonal relationships have greatly improved since taking the initiative to ask questions and act upon the answers (verbal or unspoken). To make a long story short, this man rambled on about not wanting a relationship. If *the scam* had worked, I would have given more of my attention than he deserved. To say this guy was smooth is an understatement.

Let's examine the *expert-level scam* he attempted to run next. This particular Black male had a conversation with third-party friend of mine (with full knowledge that it would get back to me). Apparently, I am so enthralling that he did not quite know what to do for me. The mating dance does not vary by much in this country. Now what man truly has no idea what to do for a woman that he's interested in? Then this con artist proceeded to ask my friend if he should get me flowers. When told what had transpired, I wanted to throw up everything eaten that day. Apparently, this man believed that I had just fallen off of the Stupid Truck onto Idiot Street. What a disingenuous way to try and condition me to be used! Kept silent and waited just in case I was jumping to conclusions. By the way, those flowers are still lost in transit.

The third Black man (thirty-one years old) was a former co-worker that I had run into. He coordinated the more popular scam called "The Mirage Date." This is the date that is put out into the ether. He promised to take me out "soon." When I attempted to get a day and time, the mirage disappeared. Funny thing though, his number was in my missed calls list showing 2 a.m. I am curious to know what was open at that hour.

The fourth Black man (thirty-two years old) offered to bring McDonald's over to my house. Enchanting as the offer was, I had to decline.

There were two men from other races that I've dated that did go "poof." However, I did not notice the level of game-playing experienced with the Black men. These two men of other races made it clear and ceased calling and returning calls. Message received and no hard feelings. Let's just say my life is changing tremendously for the better. My love life is definitely on the upswing.

Brief Synopsis of "The Scam":

- Professing not to want a committed relationship, but using every angle to cash in on the benefits. He simply slaps a disclaimer on in the beginning to justify his actions.

- Constantly involves third parties; conveys deceptive messages via a friend or, worse, a family member to make the target believe his feelings run deep—all while knowing full well that the information will get back to the target. This technique makes the man appear shy, sensitive, and vulnerable. Women, do not fall for it! Wait for that man to act. Real men bring their own lasso to the rodeo.

- Whining to his target about being "used" in the

past by the big, bad, bitter, angry Black woman. Let's pack our bags, we're going on a guilt trip! This tries to play on the Black woman's sympathies so she will not make too many demands on him. The next sound heard will be a lowball offer dropping on the table.

-Making "air ball" dates without any real intentions of following through. That date will be harder to pin down than a helium balloon. The old bait and switch is expected after this approach. Under this ruse, the date will turn into a house call complete with takeout and a video.

THE TIME IS NOW!

Tick tock, tick tock: Time's A-Wasting!

R ight now, it's about survival. We cannot afford any longer to exclusively wait for anyone Black, White, or indifferent to get their act together. Understand, sisters: *We do not have the precious commodity of years to sit around playing with men-children, wishing for things to change!* The change has to come from us. Health professionals dictate that a woman's fertility begins to decline at age twenty-seven, as reported on the Web site www.protectyourfertility.org.

"Over the past several decades, demographic and socioeconomic trends have resulted in an increase in the absolute number of women seeking pregnancy in their late thirties and early- to mid-forties. In addition, a significant number of women in this age group are seeking evaluation and treatment for infertility. Although there is a very well demonstrated decline in female fertility as a function of age, this phenomenon has typically has been under-recognized not only by the general population, but also by many health care providers. This is probably related to the fact that in previous decades, women generally had completed childbearing by the late thirties and in fact many of the pregnancies that occurred in the later reproductive years were unplanned. An increased awareness of the effects of aging on fertility for patients and health care providers is critical to the prevention of age-related infertility."

—www.protectyourfertility.org

To be perfectly clear, women of any race (especially over the age of twenty-five) do *not* have time for the following:

- Not being asked on a proper date. A call with him stammering something about getting a drink at 10 p.m. is unacceptable. Nor is waiting for the last minute to make plans. Do not accept being bookmarked; we either have plans or we don't. What would be acceptable notification in advance is a decision each individual woman has to make. Listen to instinct, not desperation.

- Some guy with a newborn. I also feel very uneasy about men on the prowl who have children in pampers.

- A man without a mode of transportation. (This does not include metropolitan areas such as New York City, etc.)

- A "concubiner." He's got kids by how many different women?

- A man who lives with momma and shows no evidence of having saved up or contributed significantly to the household.

-A man who just got a divorce and/or recently stopped living with a woman.

- A man who exhibits no clear indication of exclusivity after a reasonable amount of time. In addition, I would seriously question becoming intimate under the following circumstances:

1. If the has woman not met his family and friends.
2. If the woman has never been to his house (or, if she has, was rushed in and out).
3. If the woman has not heard any discussion or seen any actions regarding the future.

The timeframe and for relationship progression is an individual choice. Professional opinions can help put this into proper perspective. My take? Don't give sex to scum.

I witness so many of us wasting precious time with someone who should have never had any of it to begin with. Not too many things irk me more than someone who wastes time, whether it is for a business or social endeavor. It breaks my heart to see so many wonderful, smart, beautiful, educated, Black women holding out for something that may not happen. We are *not* being "uppity" (I will expand further on these adjectives used on Black women who do not comply with the Black Community Machine later) when seeking a mate at or above our level. Not seizing the opportunity and exploring all options available would be a great loss to those

quality women. Black women are conditioned to accept
Sugar,
Honey
Iced
Tea and then expected to make a gourmet meal. It saddens me to see so many Black women looking bewildered and shell shocked, seemingly with no direction or any clue to how they've gotten to this point. I am dedicated to helping Sisters raise the bar. Black women deserve love, marriage and legitimate families like everyone else in the world.

Why Black Women Deserve Better

Few have the courage to be the dissenting voice while everyone else is pretending that nothing is wrong. Many treat the state of Black man/woman relationships today as being normal. Black women in particular often shy away due to frequent accusations that label them as angry, bitter, and demanding. We cannot keep silent because there are two Black men in the neighborhood doing what they ought to do. That is simply not good enough. Black women have been cautioned subtlety and overtly against questioning The Black Community Machine's motives. We are frequently called very ugly names for speaking up. For this reason, I will not package this book in covert themes featuring non-offensive, namby-pamby titles. I want to be in everyone's face. I want Black women to get uncomfortable enough to make the necessary changes in their lives. To get their heads out of the sand and stop living life based on illusions. I want Black women to get a righteous anger within, motivating them to save little Black girls. Have the courage and fortitude to break away from the herd and its mentality. A number of Black women's quality of life will only deteriorate if left unchecked.

Black women say...

"When a Black woman is younger and has hopes of having a Black family, I think it is normal to visualize and express that. A majority of Black women have a Black man in mind. It is not until the likelihood of finding a Black man is truly gone do we start to talk about the possibility of marrying outside our race."

"But unfortunately, far too many Black women have this naive view that a Brother is by nature of being a Brother, a good man. Sometimes to our detriment, we love Brothers unconditionally. Perhaps that means loving without judging his bad behavior? Perhaps it is something caused by external forces like racism."

(I guess Black women weren't around for the racism thing.)

"My spirit gets heavy when I think of all the talent, wealth, knowledge, and other intangible resources we have as a people, and yet we remain so far behind. We do not trust, honor, respect, nor support one another. So if these statements are valid, then it would be indicative that we do not love each other."

"I am not alone! So tired of crying my eyes out trying to figure out what's wrong with me. I have wracked my brain trying to figure out why I have been having such a difficult time finding a Black mate. My esteem has tanked."

HOW BLACK WOMEN
ARE DEVALUED

Something has got to give. We are in crisis mode. Black women have been and are so mistreated, beaten down, marginalized. This is often at the hands of those who call us "queens." In my experience, these men are the ones who almost collectively treat us the worst. Basically, the actions are speaking so loudly I cannot hear a word they're saying. However, I refused to sit down, be quiet, and pretend that nothing is going on. I will stand up and display myself to the world if it means helping Black women. Especially if we have a snowball's chance in hell of saving our children (little Black girls especially) from this environment. Black women need to wake up and expand their dating options.

What in the name of all that is pure and good has happened with music? I miss the sounds of The Temptations; Earth, Wind & Fire; Marvin Gaye; Jackie Wilson; Al Green; The Isley Brothers; The O'Jays; James Brown; The Four Tops; etc. I am at the point now where the radio doesn't even get turned on anymore. Everything is "N---a this" and

"B---h that." We have the wanna-be gangstas perpetuating Black-on-Black crime. Don't forget every other variation of wanting perverse no-strings sex, without regards for consequences. When young women begin emulating these labels, people are surprisingly shocked by this. Wonders never cease.

Here is an example of the type of music no woman should ever be a part of. Black women, please turn off and immediately cease support of the TV, movies, and radio that promote derogatory behavior towards us. There is no shame in wanting no part of the twenty-first century version of a minstrel show. With all the cooning and tomfoolery to boot.

What Are Our Children Listening To?

Forget Stevie, forget Marvin, and forget Luther. Here's...

Gucci Mane: "Freaky Girl"
"Then you get some brain in the front seat of the Hummer.

Chris Brown, T Pain: "Kiss, Kiss"
"We parking lot pimpin in my donk and I know what you want."
Souljah Boy: "Crank Dat"
"Soulja boy off in dis hoe."
(Gee, I'm in the mood for love now...)

Black women say...

"Black women know that in the work world, we have to be twice as great to get half as far. Is that also true in dating? Do we have to be twice as beautiful, twice as smart, and twice as good to wind up with only half the man?"

"This should be a warning to damaged Black men that their reprobate behavior would turn society against them."

"I used to love most hip hop, but I can see clearly the damage it is destroying our communities across the country. And as a Black woman, I can't line the pockets of these 'artists' who see me as no more than a 'gold digger' and vessel for their sexual desires."

Lil Wayne Interview about hip-hop rivalry:

(Put the maternity ward on lockdown, Lil Wayne wants to murder newborns! This is what a lot our young Black boys and damaged men wish to emulate.)

Here is a direct quote:

"If you are talking about rap and beef, I'm the wrong person to talk to. I am from New Orleans. Cut your televisions on. You know where I'm from. I'm from the murder capital, ma. Beef is a different thing there. I have four teardrops on my face and I have to look my mom in her eye every day. I can't lie to her. F-ck what they think and f-ck what the world thinks, we real.

My mom is real. The first day I got a teardrop I

lied. I called her and asked her can I get a teardrop tattoo, but I had already got it. She said, 'When you get it, come by me so I can see how you look with it, cause I was thinking about getting one my f-ckin' self.'

"We don't play. No, I'm not gonna rap about you man, I will murder you, your family, your child, a newborn, I don't give a f-ck. I could never go to hell cause I'ma take over, b-tch."

—*Source:http://www.mediatakeout.com/20303/lil_ wayne_if_you_diss_me_ill_murder_your_children.h tml*

What a nice fellow! I wonder what would happen if Lil Wayne was locked in a room with the mother of a newborn whom he had threatened. Not pretty.

Black women say...

"Many Black men have abdicated their responsibilities often blaming the Black woman for neglecting their families."

"Young Black boys are given a completely different message. It seems that all that's required of them is to graduate high school and not go to prison... This is where a huge chunk of the problem is; we have low expectations of Black boys... A lot of the fathers are absent and there are a lack of *mentors*"

"Complacency develops in relationships when they feel that their partners don't have any options other than them. This is what in my opinion has occurred between Black men and Black women. The shortage of eligible Black men has created a really ugly dynamic in the Black community. Black men often take the support Black women give them for granted."

DISMANTLE THE STRAW MAN

From Wikipedia, the free encyclopedia, at en.wikipedia.org:

"A straw man argument is an informal fallacy based on misrepresentation of an opponent's position. To 'set up a straw man' or 'set up a straw man argument' is to create a position that is easy to refute, then attribute that position to the opponent. Often, the straw man is set up to deliberately overstate the opponent's position. A straw man argument can be a successful rhetorical technique (that is, it may succeed in persuading people) but it is in fact a misleading fallacy, because the opponent's actual argument has not been refuted."

I have been cursed out and had violence threatened against me for sharing my Web site with Black women. Resorting to violence is the last resort of some damaged men when their bag of tricks has failed. Forget about any attempts to defend personal choice against those who have ulterior motives for us. There is no reasoning with damaged men. These parties will throw up multiple straw man arguments in attempts to weaken the position of Black women who chose to expand their dating options. Ladies, meet the straw men:

- Black women who date interracially will not give the Black man a "chance" and hate Black men (or even themselves).

- Black women who date interracially think White (or Latino, Asian, etc.) men are superior.

- Black women believe dating outside of their race will end all of their problems. (That's called a Pollyanna. I am addressing women who are dedicated to finding love based on reality.)

- Black women have subscribed to a "White-woman feminist doctrine."

Very few women wish to be labeled as a militant bra-burning ranting and raving man-hating feminists. This is an unattractive visual often successful in making her back down.

The most popular, which makes the Black woman into a type of "straw man" herself is *the bitter and angry Black woman.* The accusation of being the bitter and angry Black woman is enough to scare most of us into submission. We dare not bring up any valid concern about Black men, especially in a public setting. Black women have been well programmed by the Black Community Machine. This straw man tends to be the most effective and accomplishes the following:

1. Silences/shames the Black from woman expressing their concerns, fears, frustrations, and opinions.

2. Addressing a Sister as **the bitter and angry**

Black woman deflects from the real issue at hand. It's a very convenient scapegoat when someone does not wish to admit to nor deal with a problem.

3. Quite often, the Black woman's past experience with damaged men will be used against her. Absentee fathers as well as previous bad experiences with men will always be her fault. On the other hand, the damaged man will advise that she is too paranoid for just those very reasons. The so-called paranoia is usually alarm bells going off. Nothing to see here, folks.

What Sherlock Knew

Most of us have watched shows or read stories featuring detectives. In order to solve the case clues were gathered and examined. Detectives depicted in the past rarely if ever became personal with the suspect. Evidence was collected in order to prove the case. One factor always taken into consideration was past behavior. History repeating itself is a near certainty. Detectives are not trained to act on their emotions or to wish things were different. The detective will present the case in court and let the jury or judge decide. Criminals have distinctive patterns when committing a crime. Most exhibit some combination of these behaviors:

- Evasiveness: Rarely answers with a "yes" or

"no" that is not usually followed by a trail of excuses.

- Offering unnecessary information to throw the other party off the scent. A good indicator of this occurring is if the thought, "Well, what does that have to do with anything?" crosses the mind.

- Lining up witnesses ahead of time: As in when the suspect introduces individuals to the story who have no real involvement.

- "Not lying": Devises a clever and distracting play on words to conceal involvement in a crime. Or in this case revealing how damaged a man is. He will never make a technically untrue statement. Yet still, he will purposely allow the receiver to draw the wrong conclusions.

- Repainting the picture: The boldface criminal will attempt to convince the detective and/or the victim that they are not actually seeing what's in front of them. The parallels run similar to people who have dirty houses. They will attempt to convince visitors that there just wasn't an opportunity to clean up today. Quite the contrary, a foul odor is thick in the air and everyone sees as my grandmother used to so eloquently put it, "Not today's dirt."

Consequently, we can learn a lot from a detective and apply it to our personal lives. Learn to ask open-ended as well as specific questions. Next ingredient, *listen closely* for inconsistencies! Most women are very proficient at information gathering while holding up their end of the conversation. Ladies, use this verbal advantage. A damaged man will more than likely answer the open-ended and closed questions differently. For instance, try one style of inquiry on date No. 1 and the other on date No. 2. Most criminals cannot keep up with their own lies. Disregard those who may accuse the woman of being a snoop, sneaky, and asking too many questions. This boils down to personal responsibility. Yes Sisters, hire a private investigator if deemed necessary. An ounce of prevention is worth a pound of cure. I certainly have done some investigating on suitors in the past, which has saved me a ton of trouble in the long run. Our very lives are at stake. I wonder how this would affect the number of exploited and missing young women seen in the newspapers, if this lesson were taught more frequently. The risks are too great in this day in age when many men cannot be counted on as protectors. Damaged men can kill!

Critical Thinking: Criminals do not like questions. How many men from the past were unreceptive when legitimate inquiries were made of them?

Why do people who say they have nothing to hide, hide everything?

Black women say...

"Find out about past behavior...That is the only way to tell whether or not the character they are projecting is authentic."

THE BASTARDIZATION OF OUR CIVIL RIGHTS MOVEMENT

Black women say...

"Black people have come a long way. Unfortunately in regards to emotional intelligence, not far enough."

Residual effects from slavery touch Black women and men alike. My biggest "Oh give me a break!" moment is when Black men whine to Black women about slavery and "the evil White man." We all have to compensate and prove ourselves to counteract the prejudice that still exists.

When the Black woman inquires about or tries dating outside of her race, immediately she gets run over by the Black Community Machine's guilt parade. The guilt parade eagerly gives her lessons in slavery and other Black history. Black men cannot get ahead in life because of "the man." The Black woman is then warned that "de evil White man" is only after sex **(as if this quality would not be found from Black men, green, or polka dot men).**

CW

I have had Black men address me as a mammy, Un-
cle Tom, bitch, White man's whore, etc., for saying
that Black women should expand their options to
include all races. These tactics are used to bring
about a strong genetic memory or emotions regarding a very shameful part of our history. It's propa-
ganda enacted to keep Black women from dating
other races. My first reaction? How dare these people mock what our ancestors endured in order to
manipulate another's choice! How dare they bas-
tardize the struggles for freedom and civil rights
into a platform for the damaged male's self-serving
interests. Civil rights leaders fought and died around
the world for all of us to exercise choice. Racism
will most likely always exist in one form or another.
There is always someone out there who will not like
your face. Life holds obstacles for everyone on the
planet.

Assimilation

"Cultural assimilation (often called merely assimilation) is an intense process of consistent integration whereby members of an ethno-cultural group
(such as immigrants or minority groups) are "ab-
sorbed" into an established, generally larger community. This presumes a loss of many characteristics of
the adsorbed group. Assimilation can be the process
through which people lose originally differentiating
traits, such as dress, speech particularities or manner-

isms, when they come into contact with another society or culture. Assimilation may be voluntary, which is usually the case with immigrants, or forced upon a group, as is usually the case with the receiving "host" group or country.

A region or society where assimilation is occurring is sometimes referred to as a melting pot. Cultural assimilation is an intense process of consistent integration minority groups into an established, generally larger ethnic community. This presumes a loss of many characteristics which make the minority different."

—en.wikipedia.org

Watch out! The somewhat educated sycophant will throw the term "assimilation" around. These are big words which can be intimidating to those who do not have full understanding. Those who do not subscribe to the brainwashing are accused of assimilating with a so-called "White America." Most minions of the Black Community Machine misuse this word. It is impossible for Black people to assimilate in the present due to the duration we have been here. Blacks were forced to assimilate in the 16th century at the beginning of slavery. Unfortunately, we had to give up many of our Afrocentric identities and traditions for obvious reasons. An American relocating to Saudi Arabia or a European country would definitely have to assimilate. America is not our host; we did not need a passport to come here. Black people *are* this country! America is our nation too due to the blood, sweat, and tears of our ancestors. Most Black people in America did not immigrate. We cannot assimilate into any entity that we already are a part of. Keeping the definition in mind, what would Black people have to assimilate into?

Last time I checked, Blacks and Whites go to the mall, supermarket, and restaurants. Our diets do not vary much from one another. Black and Whites listen to R&B, rock, blues, jazz, pop, dance, gospel, and even hip-hop. We have work, come home, do our chores, and spend time with family. Blacks and Whites go to the doctor when ill. We mourn at funerals and celebrate joyous occasions (weddings, graduations, birthdays, anniversaries, etc.). Blacks and Whites engage in recreational activities such as travel, sporting events, parties and shows. We all attend school, date, marry, have babies, visit houses of worship, and keep pets.

So again, what are we assimilating into? *There is no such thing as a Black American assimilating with America in the 21st century... Impossible!*

Critical Thinking: Black women have a knack for making a way out of "no way." A majority of us do not get caught up in excuse making and playing the race card. What is the Black man willing to do on his own to overcome?

Black women say...

"Does anyone really believe the problem of lack

of marriage or finding suitable mates among Black women is attributed to the 'pickiness' of the BF? Those who are honest about analyzing this quagmire will find the cause very easily...Basically it's BW who frequently gives BM a free pass on their pathological behavior, which should instead have been cut off at the pass and stamped out from Jump Street..."

"I would rather have a BM tell me that he is not into BW, than say that he cannot find one "on his level." That is very insulting."

"Many BW are afraid to tell a BM that she wants to get married in fear that he will flee."

(Brainwashing in full effect! It's making Black woman believe there's something inherently wrong with her desires for a legitimate family, that she is too desperate and demanding.)

"It's amazing how many BM consider themselves a good catch, yet have no intent to marry."

DAMAGED, DAMAGED, DAMAGED

Identifying the Damaged Black Man

The damaged Black man best describes men who should be avoided at all costs.

Who is he and how do we deal with him? Typical characteristics are as follows:

- Always deflects blame for his actions on a faceless entity; i.e., "The Man" (I'm sure he's out there somewhere lurking in the shadows).

- Denies that a problem exists or suggests that it is being "blown out of proportion." Belittles/ minimizes feelings.

- Looks for a woman to become a scapegoat. If she doesn't play mammy to this man's woes, look out; she will be vilified.

- Does not acknowledge the faults of his peers; Tends to zero in on the weaker vessel instead of calling his brothers out on their indiscretions. It would require courage to confront another man on his bad behavior. Damaged men are not courageous.

- Demands, pressures, and guilt-trips the victim/target into shutting up, accepting sub par treatment, and admonishes the victim to feel Blessed that it wasn't worse. After all, it was somehow the victim's fault to begin with.

- Once the target has left the aggressor and stops engaging, the damaged man will follow and harass unrelentingly to ensure continued victimization.

Never let the damaged man continuously engage, guilt, or draw you back in. Keep stepping forward with head high and dignity intact. This damaged soul will never acknowledge, empathize, or change due to any dialogue. He will have to make the decision ultimately to pull himself up by the bootstraps.

Let's Play "Damaged Black Community Machine Man-ipulopoly"

The quagmire has its roots in when the Black woman tries to please the typical damaged Black man. She cannot go left nor right because every move is the wrong one. Therefore, the question is, What is a Black woman to do? I can almost visualize this as a board game. The routine goes something like this:

-Black woman is told not to be a gold digger, not to depend on "no man" and be independent. Spin the dice...

- Black woman lands on success; i.e., schooling, getting her own place, and contributing to society. She is now looking for a Brother with the same or (gasp!) a higher level of credentials.

Pick a card... It's "the Black Community Machine," who now says she's too uppity... Move two paces back.

- Black woman lands on the "Chance For Love." Move one pace forward.

- Black woman then makes an honest effort to overlook some obvious shortcomings and give the Black man a chance (ex.: no place, no ride, baby-mama drama, chronically unemployed, history of inconsistent behavior within relationships).

Pick a "street-cred-down-ass-chick card." Move another pace forward.

- Things go bad with the brother she gave a chance to. The Black woman is now stuck with having to unload the bum and repairing the damage (altered financial status, being the mother to the child of a deadbeat father and legal troubles). Pick a card... It's "the Black Community Machine" card again. The card says the Black woman was stupid in the first place for falling for the brother... Move two paces back.

I think we all get the idea. The cycle continues similar to a bad game show. I opted some time ago to get off of that hamster wheel.

Black women say...

"Black boys' potential for greatness is not limited in the Black community... Black girls are told not to be too smart, too pretty, to show up the Black man… We can't have a decent job, further our education, and we can't do anything which will tick Black men off, which if you are a Black female seems to be damn near everything."

"When Black women provide for our own, then we are too independent and strong. So do you want the strength in Black women or whores? (Reference to the same line "BW don't know how let a man be a man.")

"Any time an entire race of men have to march at the Capitol in D.C. to take care of their children, that is certainly embarrassing and pathetic!"

"Love Letters" From the Damaged Black Man

Here is some feedback posted in response to some of my videos and blogs. Names have been removed to protect the damaged. (CW is the moniker I use online.)

"B----! (yes I did say b----!, because that is what you are), you are afraid of Black men. You scared that a brother like myself will expose of being a rape victim, or a former thug chaser. Your intellect is too easy to bash. Where are your White male supporters? (A healthy person is not going to sit around and try to reason with this damage) You can't stand it when a Black man questions you about your delusions."

"CW is getting trashed, because she has the

same traits of a racist White male who burns a cross on a Black family's lawn. She says something @#$$% up about Black men, and she runs away. I have no problems with CW hating Black men, because I hate the shyt out of Black women. I wouldn't piss on one if she was on fire. My things is that I do not mind being questioned about my hatred for Black women. I let my hate be known when I am out in public. I have been questioned about hatred towards Black women, and I answer the questions. CW doesn't have a backbone unless she is hiding behind a White guy. Black women are the ones who choose sorry A$$ Black men at a young age. Once they are used up by thugs, ballers, and cheaters, they put ALL Black men into one box."

"I be so...happy when you find your White man. but PLEASE don't keep saying the numbers are not there. Follow your heart and don't make excuses. If that is what you want to do, go for it. I am happy when you find your white man. but PLEASE don't keep saying the numbers are not there. Follow your heart and don't make excuses. If that is what you want to do, go for it. I am going to start letting Black men know where to find women that will appreciate them as well. Frankski Gave a trip to Brazil a few years ago and the women down there treated Black men the way a man should be treated. I will highly encourage Black men to go there because at least they don't act stuck up and they are EX-TREMELY beautiful." **(Authors note: I have a feeling that if these damaged men actually stayed**

for any length of time, there would be a mass exodus of Brazilian women.) "They only act phony when they come to the states and see how Black women here treat Black men. You and the rest of Black women can go ahead and do what you do but millions of other Black women have already beaten you to the punch. They have thousands of websites looking for White men so what you are saying is nothing new. Over 80 percent of Black women are looking for White men. Other races don't fit the equation. They are strictly looking for white men. The numbers are there, you just don't want to admit that they are there to justify getting a white man. Now White women on the other hand. 97 percent of them stay with White men and are proud of their men. Black women have always wanted to be White anyway. That is why they fry their hair, where wigs, change the way they talk when they get around White men, watch soap operas, take thousands of roles kissing white men, say the baby is cute if they see another Black woman with a baby by a White man, bleach their skin, look down on their men, praise White men, let White men degrade them in porn movies but talk bad about Black rappers that have them shaking their butts but still have their clothes on, wear blue, green, and grey contacts, say they are tired of being lonely knowing they are lonely because they want to be and a list of other things. But no matter how much you want to switch, you are still a N!GGER in his eyes. A n!gger that is easy to %$$@!"

Sisters, hold your own here. Do not let the damaged noise through to affect your psyche. If one of these men questions your decision to date/marry interracially, ask him the following:

1. Whom are you married to?
2. Are you planning to marry the woman you're with? Any intentions on legitimatizing a family?
3. How many of the Black men in your family are married to Black women?
4. Do you know any eligible Black men available for an introduction?

Is the silence deafening? Subject changing, with a little hemming and hawing to boot? The answer or lack thereof will bring clarity to. Nine times out of ten the subject will return to blaming Black women. Beware of people who attempt to discourage any plan in which they are not equipped to contribute.

Black women say...

"Black men define themselves by their penis size and sexual conquests. They do this when their anatomy is praised by TV, by White women and other sources. They've bought into the bill of goods that is being sold, and think their manhood is defined by the number of women that they bed and the size of their penis."

"Fear of emasculating Black men has caused us to be silent about ourselves."

"Are there any Black athletes left who are married to Black women? Michael Jordan and Shaq, I believe, have divorced (or are in the process of divorcing) their Black wives. I am a successful and educated Black woman living this nightmare."

"Black women are like toys to Black men: 'I'll play with you now and when I am bored with you, I'll toss you in the toybox with my other used up toys.' Then, when someone else wants the toy, the spoiled two-year-old comes out, 'Mine, mine, mine!' They don't really want they toy, but will be damned if they're going to give it up to anyone else who does."

"When Black men are broke they will use Black women's necks to get where they need to go...until they get there, that is..."

WHO EXACTLY IS
"THE BLACK COMMUNITY"?

The Deli

A neighborhood delicatessen had been a landmark in the community for about 50 years. Everyone *raved about their food. Approximately 20 years into operations, new management took over. Stories occasionally began circulating about customers receiving poor service. This was a good business, therefore the neighbors assumed that there was some sort of mix-up or miscommunication. Time progressed and the rumors became more frequent about this deli's increasingly poor service. Based on the businesses reputation, patrons from outside the area began visiting. Soon after, talk began circulating that the deli actually preferred the outside customers better than those within the community. Those who lived in the neighborhood were accused of being loud, argumentative, and greedy. The neighbors refused to believe that the delicatessen, which has been a pillar in the community would say such things about them. After a few years almost everyone within that*

41

circle noticed the quality of the food became extremely poor. Cheap portions, food poisoning, overpricing became the norm. The deli also began leaving their cast-offs in the street for others to pick up and take care of. On the other hand, patrons from outside the area stated that the food was great. The out-of-towners also claimed that people in the community just did not appreciate their local deli.

One day the neighborhood delicatessen posted a "Going Out Of Business" sign. The neighbors were puzzled. Prior to that there were ongoing talks and meetings to discuss problems between the neighborhood and business. The deli stated all the community had to do was "shape up". Demands included that the customers not raise their voices, question the quality of the meat or make too many complaints. The deli advised everyone that they had it rough too. Most of the neighborhood complied with the deli's requests even though the service did not change nor improve.

The delicatessen stayed on despite the "Going out of business sign". However, they mainly catered to patrons from out of town. Whenever a customer from the community came by, the doors were always locked. The times when they could get in, scraps were the only thing available.

Then surprisingly a new deli opened just on the outskirts of town. The community was a buzz, speculating on the new business. However, only a few in the community ventured out to try the new place. Their reports consisted of excitement and praise.

The few then went onto spread the good news to the others. To their amazement , the community began chastising them for going outside of "the old neighborhood". The community accused the patrons of the new delicatessen of being disloyal and undermining commerce. "But you don't understand!" The few exclaimed. "The food is excellent, service is with a smile, and the prices are fair!" The loyalists in the community told the few that everyone should keep trying to work it out with the deli that's been in the neighborhood for all these years. That it would be wrong to just stop going and everyone needs to stay strong. Suggestions were also made that the neighborhood should do more to help the business along. Not to look for an 'easy way out' of their problems with the deli. And besides, they can go on eating the poor quality of meat just a little longer. Endure being ignored for out of town customers just to show the deli how loyal the community really is...

Black women have always been encouraged to engage in the "see no evil, hear no evil" charade concerning the decline of Black men. We have been encouraged to "take it" like some mule and keep plowing. Now is the time to reject the role of being that mule or a burden-bearing mammy. Black women are not obligated to put a Band-Aid on the entire race. This is different from taking on worthy causes; i.e., activism, raising funds, mentoring, and even protests. The true civil rights leaders of yesterday and today are heroes. On the other hand, I have nothing but disdain for the well-known faces who always put on a dog and pony show for the press. These so-called Black leaders always materialize when there is a camera present. Stop supporting any venue that doesn't have our best interests at heart, even if it has a "Black" label slapped across it. Do not become a sucker for the Black Community Machine.

How many of us have ever been told the following while growing up or even now?

-"Don't give that man a hard time!" (When he's performing below standard.)

-"Chile, the Black man goes through enough living in this country. We don't need to add to *his* stress."

-"Now don't go making a big thing out of this" —being conned, cheated, raped, beat, spit upon, whatever by a damaged Black man—"there are enough brothers in jail already. "

Traits of being "mammified" woman:

-Constantly defending a man despite his being at fault, lazy, and irresponsible.

-Allowing a (way-past) adult son to live at home and contribute little to nothing.

-Supporting any able-bodied man who cannot seem to find or keep steady work.

-Bailing this same type of man out of self-inflicted situations at the expense of house, finances, and sanity.

Black women are not sacrificial lambs. Refuse to accept any further mind control from the Black Community Machine. An easy way to tell if a Black woman is being victimized by the machine is when terms such as "uppity," "feminist," "house negro," or "bourgeois" are being thrown at her. These words have very negative connotations until the Black woman does a little research. Without this knowledge, images of the well-to-do Black woman wrapped in diamonds and furs ignoring little starving children come to mind. The Sister must be of a certain mindset to deprogram. This doctrine is a very clever tactic use to quiet contrarian views, maintaining the status quo. Another plan of attack is to accuse the Sister of not being a real Black woman for dating outside of her race. How ironic; when the situation is reversed, mum's the word. There are no "Stand By Black Women" sermons being preached. Black women are abused, objectified, and marginalized daily.Where is the outcry, the picket lines and boycotts? Rarely will anyone hear our "Black leaders" directly hold Black men accountable. Instead, one will hear excuses like "preference" and "to each his own" (and only as long as certain parties benefit from that deal). The other mind-control technique is to give Black women a false sense of pride. We are taught not to express much, if any, desire for a relationship. Us "mammies" and "natural earth mothers" should be above that. Black women are expected to go on for years, or even a lifetime, without love and commitment. The Black woman will often walk on hot coals before admitting to needing or wanting companionship. Other races of women are not held to these beliefs. We have been greatly deceived and hurt by the very ones who are supposed to be our protectors.

The Black Community Machine also becomes eerily silent whenever Black women are victimized or turn up missing. This is quite strange since Black women are most often abused by a damaged Black man. Most readers will have never seen the following stories in the mainstream media. They received some attention, but in my opinion, one would have to be glued to the television set 24/7 to catch it on the crawls.

Just ask these women what damaged men can do. The ones who are still fortunate enough to be among the living, that is. Here are some stories which can be found on the Internet:

Damaged Men Can Be Deadly

Nailah Franklin - A twenty-eight-year-old Black woman, who was a successful pharmaceutical representative, was allegedly strangled and killed by her ex-boyfriend. This "gentleman" proclaimed his innocence while simultaneously posting e-mail in several attempts to cast Ms. Franklin in an unflattering light.

Daniyah Jackson - A ten-month-old angel who

died from internal injuries caused by sexual assault. The alleged suspect is her mother's boyfriend. In addition to homicide, the suspect is being charged with rape, endangering the welfare of a child, and involuntary deviant sexual intercourse with a child.

Alexis Goggins - A seven-year-old girl shot multiple times while shielding her mother from a hail of bullets, allegedly from her mother's ex-boyfriend in Detroit.

Dunbar Village - A Haitian immigrant was allegedly raped by a group of BM teens who lived in the apartment complex. Reportedly, she was also forced to perform sex acts on her twelve-year-old son. To date they have been charged with armed sexual battery by multiple perpetrators, sexual performance by a minor, aggravated battery, and armed home invasion.

Ebony Dorsey - A fourteen-year-old honor student's body was found in a tree line. The mother's boyfriend, has been charged with the crime.

Latasha Norman - A bright, upwardly mobile college student allegedly murdered by her ex-boyfriend.

The incidents occurred all within six months of each other. When will it end? Where are the marches, protests, and indignation? Far as we know to date, these women have not provoked fighting or broken any other laws. It is not entirely "the White Media's" fault. If we do not care about our own, who else will?

Critical Thinking: The Black Community Machine is often an advocate for various "stop the vio-lence" movements. Which parties commit most of the violence in communities? Who are the usual victims? What has the Black community really done lately to improve the safety of women and children?

Black women say...

"Why is it that any time Black women get rec-ognition of the challenges they've overcome, the Black community, particularly Black men, want to steal it away from them?"

"There is no shame in showing some vulnerabil-ity...Black women are just as human and have the same romantic needs as other women. Pretending otherwise is ineffective and attracts most damaged creatures that will prove how vulnerable you really are."

"These types of Black men are the weakest link...They will not 'man up' and take care of their children...Black women have been the heads of the household for several decades. We can't wait around forever griping about racism, and waiting on someone else to tell us when to feel about ourselves, because it will never happen. Black women have to take control of their environment."

For years I have seen pundits of "The Black Community Machine" admonish Black women to *hold out* for a good Black man. This always reminds me of the "Popeye" cartoon character Whimpy. He would always say, "I'd gladly pay you Tuesday for a hamburger today!" Sistas, do not get conned into waiting till the twelfth of never for fair due.

Black women have been long perceived as the "backbone" and "support" for the so-called Black community. Many are not used to us having a forum geared towards interests which do not include self-sacrificing, giving our all for "community causes", or waiting in one spot for a long duration. Changing the mindset is not the easiest thing to do. This also relates to goals i.e. losing weight, advancing professionally, amongst other accomplishments. When changing our eating habits there is an understanding that type of food, portion size, and activity level must be altered. Promotions at work bring on more responsibility, extended work commitments, and professional jealousy. Families may also get upset when making lifestyle changes. They may have been excessively dependent or had the wrong expectations of us to begin with. When Black women stop becoming the "safety net", certain people will get up in arms.

Examples of the 'Safety Net Syndrome':

-Having "always open" wallet.

-Dropping everything at the last minute for folks who never have their act together. This is often at the expense of those who keep their business intact.

-Certain parties know they can always "come home".

-Being expected to cheer others in victory, but the favor is rarely, if ever returned.

-Playing a role of "the unattractive" friend/sidekick (Whether this is real or perceived is irrelevant. Some would place a Sista in this category exclusively due to her "Blackness". Almost any woman who has lost weight or had some type of makeover can attest to this. Certain women will NOT want to hang around anymore.)

Now let me explain how this 'safety net' works when Black women decide to expand their dating options.

Recently, I took "Black Women Deserve Better" onto "Myspace" for Black women and their admirers to network. This blog shows positive images of BW/IR couples and links to similar blogs. This site is obviously for BW who wish to date interracially. Well, it didn't take long for the prevailing attitudes to kick into gear. A Black man forwarded me the infamous "Willie Lynch" letter (This is a popular tactic used by Black men to guilt Black women into submission.) This same Black man "agrees" that BW are queens and deserve all the best **BUT**...Would I change my approach? Case closed.

I also received a message from a White woman named "Annie" reference to the BWDB Myspace blog. It reads:

"Ok so I am ALL for interracial marriages, relationships, etc. But how can you discriminate within that? Isn't that what we are trying to avoid by accepting and encouraging interracial

marriages and relationships? I mean to make such a bold statement that Black Women Deserve Better and to make it very clear, who "better" is or what skin color or race is "better" is just another form of discrimination and hate. Love has no boundaries, no limits. And speaking from personal experience...my boyfriend (who is Black) is the most amazing man I have ever met and its not for his skin color, or his race. It is because of his character...which is what really matters. "

Well fancy that!

And I am sooo proud of our readers. I asked for their thoughts and what my response should be. I wanted to know if they were thinking the same thing. They've nailed this behavior right on the HEAD. Here are some replies:

"I find that the people who are offended are always the people who don't benefit from the 'exclusion'..."

"Perhaps if she weren't so worried about her boyfriend being offended, she could see the bigger picture."

"She was just dyyyyyyyyyin to tell you that she was dating a BM. WW have a vested interest in keeping us in a box too. If more BW started to date/marry non-BM that means we'll stop complaining about BM/WW relationships thus making THEIR stock go down!"

"Don't do what I do...do what I say". Excuse me?"

"It's plenty funny for a White woman to tell a Black woman about discrimination"

This is a taught behavior. For this reason, I will see to it that Black women have a forum dedicated to pursuing their own interests. Past history has shown that some do not believe in Black women having anything exclusively for them. This teaches Black women to operate in a place of fear. Fear of upsetting the applecart. We are always expected to lay down the red carpet for others though. This will cease when more BW understand the spirit in this attitude. Historically speaking, if enough tantrums, guilt trips, and dust is kicked up, then Sistas would back down and return to the status quo. Do NOT let allow the false "Black Community" to take this off course by placating, feel-good speech. This is another stall and the true motive will always surface in some form of telling BW not to change. I have never seen a knitter ask the sewing club "Why aren't you including me?" A checkers player saying to the chess message board "You are discriminating against me!". The distance swimmers telling the fisherman not to use blood worms for bait. See how utterly stupid that would be? There would be no benefit to that. But let me tell you guys who benefits in breaking up groups for BW & their admirers.

Who Benefits By Keeping BW Limited & Without Options?:

-Damaged who want to continuously use BW for endless resources, and as a parachute.

-BM who want their "harem" and "fan club" without reciprocity. The same BM do not wish to extend their love to BW, but will interfere when someone else tries to.

-WW who realize their commercial value goes down if BW are not clamoring, getting angry and fretting over BM. When Black women refuse to sit around looking jealous when BM & WW are gathered. Black women should leave any environment where they are ignored. If leaving is not possible, BW should otherwise occupy themselves. In other words, do not get 'used' to being ignored and relegated to a lower status. Do not resolve as a Black woman to remain in the shadows, unnoticed. Emphatically yes, BLACK WOMEN DESERVE BETTER.

More terms used to keep Black women in line:

Uppity

I suppose everyone knows what this means. To sum it up, an uppity person is someone who's presumptuous and taking liberties to which they're not entitled.

I suppose Black women are taking liberties in asking for a good man of any race. It is beyond our station to require more than the bare minimum. We are presumptuous in wanting to be treated like women and not disposable sperm containers. I have been called uppity many times. In my opinion "uppity" is slightly more politically correct terminology for b---h. On a side note: I am sick of these played-out movies that cast as the villain a successful Black woman who rejects the blue-collar worker. She "sees the light" near the end of the film. The two live happily ever after. The not-so-hidden message is that Black women should not be selective. She has absolutely no right to seek a mate at or above her level. Black women should simply take whatever is handed to them and be happy with it.

Bourgeoisie or Bourgeois

From en.wikipedia.org:

"Bourgeoisie - is a classification used in analyzing human societies to describe a social class of people who are in the upper or merchant class, whose status or power comes from employment, education, and wealth as opposed to aristocratic origin. Petite bourgeoisie (also Petty Bourgeoisie) is used to describe the class below the bourgeoisie but above the Proletariat.

The term is widely used in many non-English speaking countries as an approximate equivalent of middle class (found in the Communist Manifesto by Karl Marx and Friedrich Engels).

In common usage the term has pejorative connotations suggesting either undeserved wealth, or lifestyles, tastes, and opinions that lack the sophistication of the rich or the authenticity of the intellectual or the poor. It is rare for people in the English speaking world to identify themselves as members of the bourgeoisie, although many self-identify as middle class. On the other hand some would self-identify as proletarians. In reality many members of this class are transitory like Marx had originally argued. In the United States, where social class affiliation lacks some of the structure and rules of many other nations, "bourgeoisie" is sometimes used to refer to those seen as being upper class.

"Bourgeoisie is a French word that was borrowed directly into English in the specific sense described above. In the French feudal order pre-revolution, 'bourgeois' was a class of citizens who were wealthier members of the Third Estate, but were overtaxed and had none of the privileges which the aristocracy held (however many bourgeois bought their way into nobility; see Venal Office).

Bourgeoisie were defined by conditions such as length of residence and source of income. The word evolved to mean merchants and traders, and until the 19th century was mostly synonymous with the middle class (persons in the broad socioeconomic spectrum between nobility and serfs or proletarians). Then, as the power and wealth of the nobility faded in the second half of the 19th century, the bourgeoisie emerged as the new ruling class.

The French word bourgeois evolved from the Old French word burgeis, meaning "an inhabitant of a town" (cf. Middle English burgeis, Middle Dutch burgher and German Brger). The Old French word burgeis is derived from bourg, meaning a market town or medieval village, itself derived from Late Latin burgus, meaning 'fortress' or bourgeois.

"The term bourgeois is a social label applied to an individual who is seen as typical of the middle classes, both upper and lower, valuing materialism and being respectable. Exuding an image of success through consumption, personal behavior, speech and intellectual development are common attributes of a bourgeois personality. As opposed to a person with radical tendencies or one who exhibits bohemianism, the bourgeois lifestyle tends to be more traditional, centered around consumerism and activities deemed respectable by the bourgeoisie. **The term may be used with negative connotations, emphasizing the conspicuous consumption patterns, materialism and status obsession of a bourgeois mind-set**." (Author's emphasis)

If we were to believe the Black Community Machine, Black women are being bourgeois when aspiring to achieve more than the bare minimum. Keeping in line with the same mentality, we should not obtain higher education, own property, invest, look too good, or aim higher. Heaven forbid if Black women desire their men to have any of these things. She will get worked over big time by the Black Community Machine. The definitions applied here are not designed to condescend, but only to highlight how words are often misused to further an agenda.

Warning: These labels used towards Black women will become more slanderous and vicious as more begin to wake up and let their feet do the talking. The Black Community Machine will go into overtime in order to keep the Sister fearful and brainwashed. There will never be a right time to start. Sistas, we have to just pick our feet up and get going. Courage will come with action. Not every Black woman will be prepared to accept this message. The Black Community Machine lulls us into a false security by having several obviously positive mantras; i.e., go to school, stay out of jail, and don't abuse small animals. The damaged Black male is terrified that Black women will have an epiphany, which is already happening in large numbers. In the very near future Black women will walk out, lock the door, and turn off all lights on the way out. There will be no "home fires" burning waiting for him to return.

The Damaged Files...

"I hate to get mean here, but there are some Black women that are so stuck in neutral as far as their overblown self-importance and selfishness are concerned, that they believe their own bulls--t and have effectively conned themselves."

Black women say...

"BW are the only ones in this country who are

not allowed to expect anything out of a relationship."

(Or a relationship period!)

"BM are renowned for oversensitivity about
their manhood. Any words/deeds other than bowing
down at their feet is high treason."

"It is vital for Black women to be married before having children."

**Some Characters Who Help Operate The Black
Community Machine:**

-The Talking Heads: The so-called Black leaders
who never miss a chance for publicity. The exception
is when Black women are victimized by the ones who
are supposed to look out for their well-being. When
this occurs, the silence is almost deafening. With this
being said, Mr. Bill Cosby has my utmost respect for
calling out the Black community on some of these
issues. He is one of the few exceptions of those not
pandering to the same old establishment. In addition
to addressing the all-girl colleges, Mr. Cosby should
also make a point of continuing to address the Black
males of this generation.

-The Obviously Damaged Men: Many of these
men are easy to spot. Most can tell within a few
minutes if they are thuggish, without direction, and
lecherous.

-Wolves In Sheep's Clothing (The more subtle
damaged Man): These characters appear Afro-

centric, talking a good game concerning "Black Unity." They call Black women "my Sister" and "queens." Their actions often prove true intent.

- The Distinguished Brother Who Looks Good on Paper but Believes He Is Above Dating Sistas: Some of the most damaged Black men are not the ones hanging out on the street corner. They are deceptively staged at work, church, or as a figurehead in the community. This Brother has his act together in every other way: job, home, etc. (things men are supposed to do anyway). However this man often has an over-inflated sense of entitlement and feels that Black women are beneath him.

- Modern-Day Mammies: Well-programmed Sisters who regurgitate the doctrine of the Black Community Machine. This can be Mom, Grandma, Aunt or a friend. In short, a female family member who recites "mammy-talk" usually means well and has the best intentions for her loved ones. The mammy has deeply ingrained philosophies due to years of programming. She may think the self-liberated Black woman is selfish and has lost her ever-loving mind.

(Even Hattie McDaniel, who played Mammy In "Gone With the Wind," used typecast roles to put her children through college. More than likely in hopes that they would never have to be mammies.)

-Red Herring: The inanimate prop used to control anyone who has contrarian views to the Black Community Machine's agenda. These sycophants use heart-wrenching, though irrelevant, circumstances; i.e., slavery, starving children in Africa, poor people in ghettos, and pointless statistics.

Critical Thinking: Take notice of the individuals who pontificate; do the same people dedicate themselves to these causes?

Red Herring:

"A red herring is a metaphor for a diversion or distraction from an original objective. An example can be found in academic examinations, particularly in mathematics and physical sciences. In some questions, information may be provided which is not necessary to solve the given problem. The presence of extraneous data often causes those taking the exam to spend too much time on the question, reducing the time given to other problems and potentially lowering the resulting score. Red herrings are frequently used in literature and cinema mysteries, where a character is presented to make the reader/viewer believe he/she is the obvious perpetrator, when in reality it is someone far less suspect.

"Other references for the term are that they were artificial red fish that was dropped down a river to distract fishers fishing for salmon. The dummy was a bright red in colour and had a shining free moving piece on the end of it that would make it look like it was a swimming fish."

— *en.wikipedia.org*

BLACK WOMEN DESERVE BETTER

Color-struck in the 21st Century

In retrospect, it was foolish of me to believe that as an adult, I would no longer have to hear about the light skin/dark skin issue. I expected that this ignorant chapter in life would be well behind me. Boy was I wrong! Maybe upon further contemplation, the idea would have occurred to me that someone had to be instilling these damaged views in my childhood friends. Growing up, the Black boys would always pick the light-skinned girls first to socialize with. Moreover, if the young lady had long hair... LOOK OUT BARNUM & BAILEY CIRCUS! They would jump through hoops for her. I have had Black men take the liberty to stick their hands in my head looking for tracks. Is this Black Love? I seriously doubt it!

Fast forward to today where the wives of high-profile Black men have become lighter and lighter over the years. Eventually we disappeared. I'll leave it with the reader to guess what happened next.

I came across a news story about a club in Detroit. Seems the establishment threw a shindig called "The Light Skin Birthday Bash." The promotion advertised that light-skinned women were granted free admission. Now doesn't this take us back about sixty-five years or so?

Paper Bag Party

From en.wikipedia.org:
"Beginning in slavery, light-skinned Blacks were given better treatment on plantations. They received jobs inside the master's house and got to travel with the families. Many of them were educated and knew about the finer things of life. Darker-toned African Americans were forced on the fields and abused. They were not allowed to get an education or they would be punished. Light skinned Blacks are perceived to be smarter, wealthier, and happier.

"When slavery ended, light-skinned Blacks created social organizations that excluded darker Blacks. From 1900 until about 1950 in the larger Black neighborhoods of major American cities 'paper bag parties' are said to have taken place. For entrance in these organizations, many operated using the 'brown paper bag' principle. Many churches, fraternities and nightclubs would take a brown paper bag and hold it against your skin. If you were lighter or the same color, you were admitted. People whose skin was not lighter than a brown paper bag were denied entry. This is one of the ways that light-skinned Black people (so called 'High-Yellow Negroes' in the North or Creoles in the South) attempted to isolate and distinguish themselves from darker-skinned Blacks.

"Some animosity still exists between light-skinned and darker-skinned Black people in the

United States. In society today, most Blacks in higher positions have lighter skin. Most Blacks with less qualified jobs and in prison are dark-skinned. Models in Black magazines and music videos are generally light skinned."

Critical Thinking: Why are the only two entities that Black women will allow mistreatment from are Black men and certain beauty supply stores who follow Black people around, treating us like thieves?

WHO CARES ABOUT IMUS?
THE HOUSE IS BURNING!

Everyone who has access to radio, television, or the Internet heard the statements made by Imus, Michael Richards, and "Dog the Bounty Hunter." I will not jump on anyone's bandwagon and become indignant with these celebrities. The comments made by these gentlemen were very ignorant to say the least. On the other hand, most Black people have misdiagnosed the cancer symptoms. We are slowly dying. While a majority of Black America is pointing the finger elsewhere, the cancer is spreading. The rest of America sees firsthand how many Black men treat themselves and Black women. Black men address us as "hos" and other disrespectful names. Imus was only parroting the dialogue taking place in our own backyards. We enable disrespect from the rest of the world by mistreating one another. For instance, if a Middle Eastern Muslim woman was referred to in this manner there would be hell to pay. And we all know this! Black men should be our advocates and not adversaries. This is why I don't give a hot damn about what Imus, Dog, and Michael Richards are saying. It is comparable with being concerned with dust-bunnies when the house is on fire. It is laughable to hear those who support the Black Community Machine complain about other Blacks who "air our dirty laundry." Other ethnic groups must shake their heads in pity when hearing this. When a house is engulfed in smoke and flames, everyone sees it. No one has to run and make an announcement once the fire has progressed. The destruction can be seen from a distance.

ATTENTION BLACK COMMUNITY: THE HOUSE IS BURNING!

"The Black man is going around saying he wants respect; well, the Black man will never get anybody's respect until he first learns to respect his own women! The Black man needs to start today to shelter and protect and respect his Black women!"

—Malcolm X, from "The Autobiography of Malcolm X, as told to Alex Haley."

True words spoken from one of our past's great civil rights leaders.

Looking to God for Answers

Yes, I am going there! The only disclaimer I will give this passage is that it has nothing to do with my love for God. I am also far from perfect, but this does not disqualify me from pointing ongoing problems in the church. I do not believe His hand is in many of the shenanigans witnessed in Black churches. When I lacked understanding, my anger and questions were directed at God. God is awesome but still allows humans free will. After tampering with His plan, we can return to the right way of doing things. There has been an unspoken rule not to speak on the Black church's role in keeping Black women single. Where should we begin? First of all, the Bible is being used as an unwilling accomplice to the "called to be single" doctrine. From my vantage point, someone is getting a sweet deal in keeping around accomplished, bright, single Black women, with disposable funds at the ready. Call me cynical, but the absence of single Black women eternally free to cook dinners, volunteer endless hours, tithe, and run a gambit of ministries would leave many in a lurch. Hiring out these services would cost a fortune. This is another example of a situation where we all need to ask, Who benefits? Single Black women are often afraid to question this arrangement for fear of being rebuked. Is being a satisfied single the missing commandment? If the questions become too frequent and too loud the "singleness is a gift" mantra is crammed down her throat. In addition, her faith in God is questioned for "making an idol" out of marriage. From personal experience, this is a major contributor to church hurt. Single women are often made to feel guilty for having an education, career and a place to lay her head at night. Otherwise, where would she live? I do not anticipate church leaders raising up to demand that single men take on a wife and stop procrastinating. God ordained marriage. The directive from Him to "be fruitful and multiply" comes to mind. It's the world that has perverted His plan into a "forever satisfied single" doctrine. We should all pray for God's direction, especially when making life-altering decisions. However, He will not send a mate via air courier. Singles must get moving! Another deception is that single Christian women have to jump through more flaming hoops than circus tigers in order to be deemed worthy of a spouse. Each book, sermon and seminar will place another obstacle in the way of marriage. The following list of actions includes great character builders in themselves; however, they appear to be used as stall tactics. Here are some of the "go throughs" which are set before single Christian women:

- -Sanctification
- -Purification
- -Trials by fire
- -Fasting
- -Waiting on the "breakthrough"
- -Learning the art of "submission." Practice with dad, pastor, employer, neighbors, male dog, and the grocery boy
- -Learning to be content with just the Lord

- -Continuously exorcising the cemetery called

"the past"

-Do more volunteer work

-Endless singles conferences that usually costs $50 and up a head. How much money do Black women spend on these things? Figure in lodging, gas, food, and purchasing supplemental materials relevant to the conference, and someone is making a mint

-Working with youth groups, taking on babysitting, and holding other people's infants to quell the desire for your own

-Reading more books advising the Christian woman to do all of the above again

The cycle never ends. That leaves Black women in their thirties, forties, and even fifties (yikes!) still waiting on God to deliver a Christian man in a sanctuary with little to no men. There is a popular Christian author who has put out several "Waiting on the Lord" books. She is a Black woman in her forties and has been waiting for a mate since I've began reading her books in the late 1990s. Sometimes I wonder if she is waiting for a Christian Black man in her church to rise up. Or is it something a bit more sinister? Is her spiritual head endorsing this endless waiting rhetoric? Years pass and Black women believe they are not married due to lack of preparation and sanctification. A light bulb went off when at thirty-one, I am hearing the same "Wait for the Lord" messages preached ten years ago. As grains of sand slip through the hourglass, so do

Black women's childbearing years.

I attended a church conference over the summer in search of answers. My expectations were raised as I read the promotional materials. "Know how to work it, while remaining virtuous!" said the flyer. Eagerly, I paid $55 for the two-day event. Looking forward to hearing a Word, I made sure to be there on time and sat front and center. There were speakers scheduled to share a revelation to us single Christian gals. When my girlfriend and I arrived, the atmosphere told a different story. Not a man in the room. Well, there were the two men that have been attending the church, in my estimation, for the past twenty years. Those gentlemen appeared to be half asleep anyway. No Brothers anywhere in sight to impart wisdom of these saved, sanctified, and from what I can tell, wonderful Sisters. One woman, an ex-prostitute, gave excellent testimony on self-respect. Besides that, there was just a lot of screaming, crying, praying and not a whole lot else happening. I do not presume to know how God feels, but I did not feel His spirit. In no way am I blaming Him for our state of affairs. Our lack of diligence and following His word led us off track. Nonetheless, I often wonder how we got to this point. There are so many questions which hang in the air. When exactly did so many men depart the church? Did the actions of women drive them out? Lack of male leadership? Or is it overbearing guilt for not manning up? I guess this is the chicken and the egg riddle. Many Black men have not only abandoned the home, but their place in the sanctuary as well.

A few verses for those who believe that God is behind the "singleness is a gift" movement (courtesy of BlueLetterBible.com; emphasis added):

Biblical References

Gen 1:22   And God blessed them, saying, **Be fruitful, and multiply**, and fill the waters in the seas, and let fowl multiply in the earth.

Gen 1:28   And God blessed them, and God said unto them, Be **fruitful, and multiply**, and replenish the earth, and subdue it: and have dominion over the fish of the sea, and over the fowl of the air, and over every living thing that moveth upon the earth.

Gen 8:17   Bring forth with thee every living thing that [is] with thee, of all flesh, [both] of fowl, and of cattle, and of every creeping thing that creepeth upon the earth; that they may breed abundantly in the earth, and be **fruitful, and multiply** upon the earth.

Gen 9:1   And God blessed Noah and his sons, and said unto them, Be **fruitful, and multiply**, and replenish the earth.

Gen   And you, be ye **fruitful, and multiply**;

9:7   bring forth abundantly in the earth, and multiply therein.

Gen
17:20   And as for Ishmael, I have heard thee: Behold, I have blessed him, and will make **him fruitful, and will multiply him** exceedingly; twelve princes shall he beget, and I will make him a great nation.

Gen
28:3   And God Almighty bless thee, and **make thee fruitful, and multiply thee**, that thou mayest be a multitude of people...

Gen
35:11   And God said unto him, I [am] God Almighty: **be fruitful and multiply**; a nation and a company of nations shall be of thee, and kings shall come out of thy loins...

Gen
48:4   And said unto me, Behold, I will make **thee fruitful, and multiply thee,** and I will make of thee a multitude of people; and will give this land to thy seed after thee [for] an everlasting possession.

Lev
26:9   For I will have respect unto you, and **make you fruitful, and multiply you**, and establish my covenant with you.

(Note: I think God wants us to be fruitful and multiply.)

Pro 18:22   **[Whoso] findeth a wife** findeth a good [thing], and obtaineth favour of the LORD.

Gen 2:24   Therefore shall a man leave his father and his mother, and shall **cleave unto his wife**: and they shall be one flesh.

Mat 19:5   And said, For this cause shall a man leave father and mother, and shall **cleave to his wife**: and they twain shall be one flesh?

Mar 10:7   For this cause shall a man leave his father and mother, and **cleave to his wife**...

Eph 5:31   For this cause shall a man leave his father and mother, and shall be **joined unto his wife**, and they two shall be one flesh.

Is anyone beginning to see a pattern?

I urge our church leaders (especially in the Black church) to consider making some changes:
-Teach that it is not wrong to desire marriage. In fact this is need which reflects the relationship between Christ and the church. Discourage the "Single and happy" doctrine. In fact, make marriage a priority. Do not allow singles to meander or be repri-

manded for wanting marriage.

-Challenge the men in church to take a stand. The married men should be an example to the single ones. Do not allow the men to continuously reap the benefits of church singles groups. Some men will use these groups to maintain strings-free contact and companionship with single Christian women. Without accountability, these men will have little to no incentive to make a commitment. This is the flip side to Christian singles groups where the women are portrayed as desperate man-eating pariahs. Pastors and other spiritual heads ought to make sure singles programs direct their participants towards marriage.

-Form men's groups preparing attendees to assume leadership. Women and youth cannot follow if there is no head.

-Counsel singles in the congregation to terminate relationships which are not leading to marriage.

Black women say...

"I'm pretty sure the devil is ecstatic with BW blaming the singleness rate on God's Will. Think of all the frustrated, lonely, and depressed women who will believe it is His fault!"

"The years quickly go by...twenty-five turns into twenty-nine, thirty becomes thirty-five...and so on."

"A woman can encourage, support and complement a man's vision. She cannot raise him. He has to be a man first and foremost."

"Black mothers have coddled and made excuses for Black men so long...There is no pressure for them to aspire to socially acceptable goals in order to have a woman."

The Damaged Files:

"By the time intelligent Black men get into college, we have been surrounded by loud, ignorant females, and expect exactly that from our Sisters. That's why we go for the other races, because we are no longer used to being attracted to Black women. Try to prove that you aren't just another Black woman; because that is what we assume."

MYTHS AND
FEARMONGERING

While browsing on the Internet I ran across blog discussing interracial relationships. The moderator called it the "Something New Movement." It bears saying that including all races for viable marriage candidates is a life decision. This is a numbers game and Black women emphatically need to increase the odds in theirfavor. This is not simply, "Go out and find a non-Black guy/live happily ever after." It is really so much more than that. Some contrarians attempt to make BW interracially dating only about White men. Last time I checked, there were plenty of other races/ethnicities. Black women must not only expand their dating options, but also cease tolerating disrespect. We cannot wait for the Black community, the Black man, nor the media to stop treating and portraying us in a negative manner. This is the point where the rubber meets the road, and actions speak louder than words. Keep your money, time, sex and other resources out of damaging arenas.

Here's where the fear tactic came in: In this particular blog, the Black woman was admonished to be aware of ulterior motives from the man of an-other race. On the surface, some of this advice can *seem* pretty reasonable. No one wants to be hurt, after all. The reader just needs to question the source (or the source's source) of this information. To me, this blog post spewed a bunch of recycled stereotypes in order to encourage BW *not* to change their way of thinking. I am always suspicious of people/entities who make a whole noise concerning change and then always remain in the same spot. The presenter makes the listener *believe* that the focus for change is being considered. But this is often a ploy to distract the parties who seek change with "busywork"—basically, discussing the issue over and over again without any action taking place. Soon the spirit will become so exhausted from defending a position, there's no energy left to actually doing anything about it. Do not sit around debating these people, because they are usually not receptive. Sistas, put the plan into motion!

Of course the slavery routine was introduced as a reason not to date interracially. None of us reading this book were even thought about when slavery was legal. It is safe to say that any man or woman alive in 2008 did not have anything to do with slavery. If the shameful chapter of slavery does not get the Black woman to submit, then let's get Mammy on the case.

Mammy says: "Chile...now you get these 'something new' thoughts outta your pecker-head...The weak, meek, humble, ones succumb…Black women need to be strong!"

Tactic No. 12: Make the parties opting for change sound like some type of cult. Some will use phrases like "drinking the Kool-Aid."

Tactic No. 34: Put the notion in Black women's heads that her non-Black man may be a closet racist. This closet racist supposedly gets with a Black woman to carry out his prejudiced fantasies. (*Ooooh baby!*) I supposed this rubbish is said to invoke images of the man tying the BW up and making her play slave-reindeer games.

This is why it is vital that Black women limit discussion with others and behave in their own interests. She will learn to trust her own instincts and stop relying on irrelevant sources for validation.

Myth: Our choices are limited because no one but a Black man would want us.

Myth: We are being disloyal to the Black Community Machine. Do not take responsibility for an entire community. Especially one that no longer meets our needs.

Myth: White men (fill in blank: Asian, whatever) only want us for sex/fetish.

Myth: Black women could never be happy without a Black man.

Black women say...

"BW are never warned about BM's ulterior motives. To some, every Brother is a knight in shining armor with good intentions. Right! Pretty much everything that can be said about WM can be said about BM, including closet racism."

Cui Bono: Who Benefits?

Critical Thinking: When seemingly irrelevant third parties take an inordinate amount of interest in who Black women date, we must ask ourselves some questions. Mainly, who has the most to gain from a particular outcome? Who would benefit from seeing change? Who has an interest in not rocking the boat?

-The Black woman exclusively dates Black and will not expand her options. This is not due to personal preference, but due to fear of the unknown and outside influences.

Who benefits?

-Keeping that in mind, the same group of like-minded Black women feels compelled to stick with Black men. Particularly when the odds are usually about 7:3 (the women outnumbering the men), it has not dawned on these women yet to broaden their horizons.

BLACK WOMEN DESERVE BETTER

Who benefits?

-Take a good look at our Black colleges. I've heard about Black men stating they can have at least five women at one time. There is little to no pressure or motivation to treasure a Black woman. In addition, the Black women who allow this are of no help either.

Who benefits?

-Black women are made to believe men of other races do not find us attractive.

Who benefits?

-Black women feel as if they have to share the Black man due to the shortage of quality Black men.

Who benefits?

-These Black women allow the Black man to lay up, father children, eat her cooking, and use up her other resources without a commitment.

Who benefits?

Truly, life is short, and men are plentiful. Never let the Black Community Machine convince you otherwise. Especially when so many brothers are running around choosing just that: otherwise. The agenda is to keep Black women in a state of loneliness, depression, confusion, and constant struggling. Anyone in this condition is far easier to control, manipulate, and use. It's like shooting fish in a barrel. When a person or group is finally convinced of their inferiority, there is no incentive to do right by them.

I have had some very revealing conversations with non-Black women. They are beginning to wake up and realize that many Black men use them solely for skin color. Suspicions begin to arise when the Black man does not have *any* White friends whatsoever. After a certain duration, It also becomes obvious the Black man feels that he has "arrived" once he is with a non-Black woman. These women begin questioning why some Black men are overlooking very good-looking, competent, and cultured Black women. The non-Black women then realize that something is starting stink in Denmark. And whether one is being included or ostracized due to skin color alone, it is not a good feeling.

Critical Thinking: How can a Black man truly love a White woman on the debased reasoning that he has "arrived" once having her?

Black women say...

"Some White women have a superior attitude

when they are with a Black man. It's not their fault. Black men often inflate their minds to make them feel they are more valuable than Black women."

More Damaged Black Man Fan Mail...

"You are one sick Black woman. Some people might say you are a racist White male, but I know you are typical nappy-headed h0. You better get your racist White male counterparts out here. You need someone to hide behind, because I am going to drop some logic bombs on your pathetic A$$."

"So, you're one of those Black women who think you're too good for a Black man."

"It is co-signing for Black women like you to leave us in the cold for White men. The media is a big help in the promotion of the flight of Black women to the white man. It works in every country that Blacks and whites live. At the rate, the media promotes Black women lying with White men and Black Women feeding into it will be destroyed in a few short generations from now and that is a bad thing. how can you mix 12 well really about 7 percent of the population with the rest of the population without destroying the probably 7% population of Black women in the United States. I do hope that Black women see the truth. They are being used to destroy Black men. You might not believe me but I am telling the truth. I love Black women and I know you don't believe me but I do if I didn't, I would not even be on your page saying nothing to you. Most of the no good Black men don't give a damn about Black women that is why they don't care if yall go to the other side but I do and I don't care what nobody says."

"The majority of White men who date Black women must either be racist or desperate as hell. You know once you are getting a Black woman who hate Black men, she was probably raped by a few thugs, cheated on by a dude on the DL, or she received an STD from a Black dude who was in and out prison. If I was a White dude, I would stay clear of Black women who throw themselves at me. "

"Black men must teach their sons from a very early age that in all honesty, Black women are NOT the best choice for them...and not waste the years of his youth in a relationship that will go nowhere... "

"My Korean queen, our daughter and I spent the holidays in France. It was not our first trip to France but I decided to visit other areas of Paris that regular tourists do not see. Thousands of Blacks live there and the Black women look terrible, worse than spooks. Black women are not trophies in France, in fact the furthest thing from it. I ski regularly and doubt if I see any Black women on the slopes. If I do, I will push them over the mountains and cheer as they fall to their death. That would make my day big time."

Damaged BM Personals

These are real personals that I have come across. Ladies, we are not missing much in regards to the Black men who reject Black women anyway.

BLACK WOMEN DESERVE BETTER

These ads are truly superficial to say the least:

SNOW BUNNY SNOW BUNNY SNOW BUNNY - 25

"Are there any (sexy) White women out there that affiliate themselves with handsome, hood rich, well endowed Black men?......if so send a pic"

TIRED OF THE BULLS---! SBM SEEKS SWF - 38

"If you ladies are tired of games, lies and players!!!! Email me your picture and tell me about yourself...I am easy going honest person....I enjoy cooking ,reading & web hunting. looking for SWF under 120lbs with a firm 34" top."

"A PROFESSIONAL Black male that is really in to White chicks ...I am in touch with the streets and even came from that life and am starting to make something out of it ...I am very sexual as all men are but I AM OPEN MINDED I wish I had a friend with benefits so I can have fun fulfill needs and still focus on my goals but some women are shallow and want you to drop life just cause they have a piece of you know what...."

I Wanna Be A White Woman's Slave

"BM ISO dominant White woman that would not mind having a slave... I know it sounds strange but I constantly have these fantasies about being a White woman's negro slave...If you're a White woman and want me to scrub & clean your house while calling me a n!@#$r over and over again"

Well Known (Or Maybe Not) BF Interracial Couples

Quite naturally this list isn't all-inclusive. Their status may have changed since this publication. This information is provided to quell the disbelief that men of other races do not want Black women for mates, or to be seen with us.

-Paul and Crystal Wall
-Sebastian and Eunice Deisler
-Gabriel Aubry and Halle Berry
-Michael Nilon and Garcelle Beauvais-Nilon
-Matt Stone and Angela Howard
-Bill Wolff and Alison Stewart
-Tom Verica and Kira Arne
-Spencer Ling and Christine Amertil
-Luc Besson and Virginie Silla
-Prince Maximillian of Liechtenstein and Angela Brown
-Brian Kleinschmidt and Erica Dunlap
-Paul Oscher and Suzan-Lori Parks
-Robin Thicke and Paula Patton
-John Venners and Angela McGlowan
-Mats and Lydia Carlston
-Ronald and Lois Betts
-Dave Davis and Lori Stokes
-Johan van der Westhuyzen and Hlubi Mboya
-Tim Adams and Sherry Saum
-Stone and Debra Phillips
-Kerry Elsdon and Gerry Rantseli

-Troy Beyer and George Lucas
-Fred Giuffrida and Pamela J Joyner
-Troy Garity and Simone Bent
-Ben Masters and Tracy Ross
-Don LaFontaine and Nita Whitaker
-Marco Aquilar and Rynthia Rost
-Jo Charlesworth and Claire Hope-Ashitey
-Max Herre and Joy Denalane (Afro-German singer)
-Clint and Dina Eastwood
-Iggy Pop and Nina Alu
-Peter and Eileen Norton
-Brett Ratner and Serena Williams
-Sam Watters and Tamyra Gray
-Marc Bolan and Gloria Jones
-Bruce Sudano and Donna Summer
-Ace Young and Essence Atkins
-Mick Jagger and Martha Hunt
-Lennie Hayton and Lena Horne
-Sam Behrens and Shari Belafonte
-Neely Tucker and Vita Gasaway
-Roger and Chaz Ebert
-Former Defense Secretary William Cohen and Janet Langhart Cohen
-David Moscow and Kerry Washington
-Roderick Spencer and Alfre Woodward
-Debra Wilson and Cliff Skelton
-Mark Bamford and Suzanne Kay
-Karlheinz Bohm and Almaz
-Keith Britton and Zoe Saldana
-David Brenner and Tai Babilonia

-Ivan and Tanya Sergei
-Luca and Oluchi Orlandi
-John Brecher and Dorothy Gaither
-Brian Gibson and Lynn Whitfield
-Justin and Kiesha Chambers
-Graham Pratt and Leslie Uggams
-William MacDonald and Eartha Kitt
-Martin Schuermann and Julie Brown
-Mark Schenkenberg and Robin Givens
-Erwin Bach and Tina Turner
-Opal Stone and Ron Perlman,
-Timothy Fales and Josephine Premice
-John Pratt and Katherine Dunham
-Mel Levantahl and Alice Walker
-Fred Viebahn and Rita Dove
-Robert DeNiro and Grace Hightower
-Boris and Barbara Becker
-Wolfgang Puck and Gelila Assefa
-Brian Musso and Heather Hedley
-Jeff Fietjens and Aisha Tyler
-Martin Sayles and Ruth Pointer
-David Bowie and Iman
-Robert Dobrish and Elizabeth Roxas-Dobrish

One of the biggest myths that will be soon dead in the water is that men of other races do not find Black women to be viable options for committed relationships. The Black Community Machine attempts to paint lurid, back-alley scenarios when other races show interest in Black women. Please visit my blog and the others listed at the end of this book for photos of high profile and "ordinary" couples who are in committed relationships. These contain wonderful resources for Black women.

SEPARATE REALITY FROM "THE WARM FUZZIES"

The message of "Black Unity" gives all good people the warm fuzzies. However, this is not what I and many other Black women have been experiencing within in our environment. There is a disparity between what would feel good, and feel great to happen and what the cold, hard reality is. Most of us born in the 1960-70s grew up with images from Black family sitcoms or hearing the voices of popular balladeers singing their love for Black women. Where can this generation turn to find contemporary positive role models? Black women cannot hang onto the past when things were different. She cannot allow valuable time to slip through her fingers "keeping hope alive."

Self Help Only Helps Self, Can Only Help Self and No One Else

Analogy Of Most Self-Help Books:

During a pilgrimage, a bicyclist's tires both go flat while pedaling uphill. He pulls to the side of the road and fixes only the back tire. The bicyclist starts again to make the journey up the hill. Several failed attempts later the frustrated biker gets angry and blames the back tire for failing him. Yet again, he only puts air in the back tire expecting to success-fully make it up the rugged terrain. The bicyclist does not understand his lack of progression.

This accurately describes most self-help books. The focus is mainly on women preparing, reinvent-ing, and altering themselves. There are a plethora of self-help books geared towards Black women. We have more than eagerly accepted the challenge of improving the quality of our lives and others. Rarely do self-help gurus tackle the proverbial head instead of the tail. Much to our dismay, many of these books provide little to no answers to the cur-rent dilemma of Black male/female relationships. The information tends to be a recycled merry-go-round of, at best, mediocre advice. The core truth is that individuals can only change themselves. Im-proving negative behaviors can help somewhat in how others respond to you. I do not want to dis-count anyone taking a closer look at themselves and making needed changes.

These resources can only take the Black woman but so far in relating with a man. We cannot change the behaviors of Black men by reading self-help books and following steps one through ten. Books of this genre are usually wonderful resources for couples who are equally yoked. Both the man and

the woman will need to be engaged. The man cannot have one foot out the door. He will not come
"home" based on the hand-holding techniques
which a majority of these books suggest. With most
self-help platforms, Black women are distracted
with never-ending self-improvement, people pleas-
ing, and a focus on what cannot be changed. She
will not slow down long enough to evaluate the
situation for what it usually is. At the risk of over-
simplifying, the only way is to encourage good cir-
cumstances/behavior and reject anything to the
contrary. I have long stopped buying into the many
deceptions that leaves many sisters in a wet paper
bag prison. Keep looking for answers in search of
that "aha" moment. Dedicate oneself to a continued
journey for truth.

-We don't need no more loosening (except for
any self-inflicted bondage).

-Who cares what planets they think men and
women live on?

-If you do not know how to love a Black
woman, then I cannot help you.

-I doubt many women period, let known Black
women, are 100 percent single and satisfied.

-Having no more, or less sheets will not eradi-
cate the problem.

-Don't need anyone else telling me I've made
bad choices in the past. Who hasn't?

Do Not Take Up Residence in a Ghost Town or Graveyard

Many Black women at some point in their lives have visited the cemetery looking for life. We tried to make it with half a man and failed miserably. More than likely, these men were alive physically but dead in every other way. Sisters, we deserve a man who is alive, involved, committed, and present. The lack of availability in our area does not mean we should give up on him. Do not be swayed by the popular slogans about learning first to be "one with yourself." We are created by God to desire relationships. I am not referring either to being a clingy, weak woman who cannot move forward without handholding. We should be well rounded with the ability to discuss a variety of topics and find our own entertainment. Black women are often spoon-fed feel-good mantras and psychobabble. How many have heard advice to the effect of, "you have to be one with thine self before a mate will come"? Or, "there is still a good Black man out there for you." To me, this is equivalent to searching for survivors after Chernobyl. There were a few, but one has to wonder what risks were taken for the search and rescue. Black women should not have to tread through nuclear waste to find the three good Black men in their neighborhood. On the flip side, do not be deceived into accepting an incomplete man out of loneliness and frustration. Black women have been deceived in to thinking that we should be ashamed of being accomplished.

The Black Community Machine gives Black women who are educated, beautiful, talented, self sufficient, and involved with their community bad press. This warped perception is about as queer as a blue fire truck. We are not a liability for having ourselves together. Any man who has a woman like that should be proud. Some Black men love to fall back on the "she's too independent" excuse. As if supporting oneself is a crime. No one is advocating being a braggart, either. A real man who is doing what he should is not so easily threatened. Americans create opportunity and wealth by pooling our resources and working together. Instead, we have women who feel they need to hide their accomplishments in order not to intimidate a Black man. Been there, done that. In the past, I have presented my career and living situation in a shroud of mediocrity to get a foot in the door with some guy. I along with other Black women have uttered vague job titles such as secretarial, office assistant, or working "somewhere in the building." These positions are not as formidable as management, executive, administrator, or anything else requiring a degree. Our little girls are counting on us to teach them that success is a wonderful thing, not a burdensome stone. Young girls pick up so quickly on our interactions with men. Do not be deceived! If we do not raise standards, these young women will not strive for better. They will observe us going through all of the schooling, hard work, and sacrifice only to wind up alone or supporting dead weight. The message will be crystal clear: Why bother succeeding at anything in life? Ashamedly, I have also skirted around the issue of my accomplishments. It is a sad day when a Black man is intimidated by a woman who owns not a mansion, but a two-bedroom townhome and has a city job. I have since resolved to stop this madness. Somehow, we have gotten off track. A Black women settling for a sub-standard man is alone anyway. A ghost town can be vacant or filled with dead men walking. If the Black woman stays there, she will become one of them.

Black women often hear damaged men say, "When I was broke, no Sister wanted to go out with me!" You bet your sweet bippie! This type of man either wants the Sista to support him or live in a cardboard box. This is a popular guilt mechanism of the Black Community Machine and it is a pile of rubbish at that. To cut the straw man off at the pass, we are not referring to wanting a BMW owner as opposed to a Nissan owner. The point being, a man who desires a serious relationship should be prepared for the responsibility of one.

A man of quality knows that he needs to bring something to the table. When that man is not able to provide, he accepts the situation for what it is. What normal person expects to gain any special favor while being broke? Those who are rational thinkers know that when money is tight, certain things will temporarily have to be cut out. Entertainment and other extravagances are reduced or eliminated during this time. Food may also get cut down to the basics. We do not expect steak and seafood dinners when funds are low. However, the damaged man will still expect quality women to give their all in all when he is not capable of providing. Women are not "gold diggers" for expecting men to have the capacity to provide. It is called being smart. Do not buy into his sob stories about how Black women have attitudes, will not give him the time of day, nor are accommodating. This male is more than likely upset due to foreseeing the free ride coming to an end. This relates to the mate selection process women undertake. Will this man now, or in the near future, be able to provide for a family? If he is "broke without a cause," then the Black woman has every right to keep looking. It seems to be easier these days to appeal to the lowest common denominator, rather than stepping up the ol' "A-Game." Sad to say that many men have chosen this route rather than thinking of the long term. When did drive and determination get replaced with insecurity and utter laziness?

The Damaged Files...

"BW should reach back and help a Brother."
(What could absolutely be more wrong? One should always strive to attain excellence rather than asking others to dumb down and lower the bar.)

Step back, slow down, and lower standards. Is this sounding familiar to anyone? The man should be the one leading his family into purpose. A Black woman's home, heart and happiness aren't a charitable foundation. We cannot claim a broken heart on our tax returns. Her children's legacy is at stake. I refuse to be a "stepping stone" for anyone who does not share the same level of commitment and worth ethic.

Critical Thinking: If a Black woman has made her career niche and owns property, why pair up with someone who is just finally deciding to get serious in their life? If this man is in his late twenties to thirties, what has he been doing all this time?

Black women say...

"If Mammy is what the BM wants...then he should go to the library and check out a copy of "Gone With the Wind.""

"If they dislike BW so much, why do they concern themselves with the other races Black women are dating? They keep throwing the 70 percent statistic in our faces. Then when Black women say 'fine, great, I'll go elsewhere,' BM gets all up in arms...""

"My role as a woman according to the Word is a 'helpmeet'. Many Black men expect a 'do all.' "

"Stay ignorant, broke and unemployed, and you

too can get a Black man. We shall overcome!"

"I have been often called the 'dream girl,' then unceremoniously dumped...So far as Black men go we're either too good or not good enough..." *(Were these men lying then or lying now?)*

"Black people are always saying that girls are harder to raise...Maybe because they are neglecting to teach the boys anything."

"If this generation of BW doesn't wake up, start dating, and marrying up, what do you all think it's going to be like for these young girls coming up? The horrors that lie in store for them... Those girls are going to be prey. Reality on what's going to happen if things don't turn around."

Family: Can't Live with Them...Can't Dump Them Off in a Foreign Country

When making a lifestyle change, one often comes under scrutiny from family members. Families tend to hang on to similar beliefs and traditions. The Black woman may be the first one to date outside of her race. There will be some relatives who will not approve of the decision. One must be prepared for a less than enthusiastic response. This is quite natural however; the individual's decision must be respected. The Black woman may elect to discuss her feelings with family while understanding that some will try and change her mind. Others will even go so far as to try and sabotage the relationship. Black women must understand that the strongest opposition may come from the ones she loves most. She must not be deterred from being with a good man, no matter what his color. Give loved ones time to get used to the idea. I have discovered that most people will come around in time. With that being said, the Black woman should make it clear that her best interests will always come first. This can understandably be a bit more delicate when dealing with senior family members. We can always value the wisdom and guidance of elders, but the decision remains ours.

FREEDOM FROM THE MACHINE

The chances for meeting quality men are greatly reduced when Black women opt to limit themselves to just Black men. It is basic mathematics that by increasing the pool of men, odds of success are greater. Irrefutably, there is a problem with Black woman/man relationships. It's not exclusively up to the Black woman (as implied by many) to fix it all and we will not continue to take on that burden. The illusion of "Black Love" is not a good enough reason to limit oneself. When a Black woman travels and moves up the corporate ladder, she will naturally meet a wider variety of people. Her chances of dating and subsequently marrying outside of her race increase greatly. Black women do not have to argue nor justify their personal choices. There is always someone who will attach negative motives to your decisions. Do not respond to these attacks directly and better yet, ignore them. Continue marching forward. Black women are the change that is needed in this world. It will not come from any "savior" in human form. There is a wonderful and liberating feeling that comes along with allowing yourself to choose. It's called freedom!

Knowing that she's free to choose, a Black woman will soon think and act outside of the box the Black Community Machine has attempted to place her in. A Black woman will not feel obligated to put up with deal-breaking behavior due to a shortage of an eligible pool of men. We are not excluding Black men, but he does not get a "pass" for being a Brother. The pressure is off to date or continue seeing someone who is not cutting the mustard or deserving. Black women need to look out for their own happiness and well-being. We deserve the best lives possible. Don't let anyone say otherwise. The pressure is off to maintain this "strong Black woman" image. We can just be women.

What Black Women Are Encouraged to Do Right Now

Some people can accomplish great change in a short amount of time. Others move in baby steps. There is no wrong or right way. Everyone is different. Commit to change. When people stay in a box, their world grows smaller as time progresses. The change many Black women need to make goes beyond dating. Expanding options applies to every facet of life. Based upon my own experience, these actions will increase confidence, awareness, and personal strength. Take control of your life!

-Make a point of learning about cultures. Dine at different restaurants with cuisine from other cultures.

-Learn about home security and self-defense. Take classes on the subject. Research the laws of gun ownership.

-Explore arenas outside of the usual environment. Peruse shopping centers, museums, and other social avenues. Go to the post office, get a passport, and plan that trip. Make a point of subscribing to a publication with local events. Participate in an activity that catches the eye. One excellent resource is Meetup.com. This site makes it easy sign up for different activities in the member's local area. Best of all, It's free to join most events. I often sign up for speed dating and conferences. My goal this year is to try attending a wine tasting, business networking event, and functions supporting charitable causes.

-Go on plenty of dates! Speed dating, singles mixers, conferences, etc. Date three or more men at once, as much as your schedule can handle. Join an online dating service; i.e., TrueDate, Match.com, Chemistry and JDate. The questionnaires and verification checks on some sites are at times annoying, but a necessary evil in my opinion. Just make sure to set aside half an hour to an hour for a profile setup. There are no guarantees. However, the probability of the men being serious and who they say they are is greater when the screening process is more involved. Be sure to have an updated, flattering, smiling photo ready on CD or on the PC. If the man asks, let him know that you are meeting different men. That will let him know that the Sister is not a tarantula, and he is not going to be lunch!

Some Suggested Icebreakers for Personal Ads

Headlines similar to the following will let men know the Sister is open to interracial dating without sounding like an ad for a bad porno movie ("Chocolate Seeking A Scoop Of Vanilla 4 A Hot Fudge Sundae": No, No, No!)

"Engaging Black Woman Seeks Wonderful Man of Any Race"

"Black Woman Looking to Meet People from All Backgrounds"

"Race/Ethnicity Not an Issue: Black Woman ISO Quality Man"

In addition:

-Cease any acceptance of disrespect. This can be as simple as walking away, no longer responding to negativity, or not fueling the fire. Sometimes defending oneself is exhausting to the spirit because the aggressor is not likely to change. Black women should let their feet, dollars, and actions do the talking.

-Sisters, are kind to one another. Do not look at other Black women as competition. It's fine to say "hello" to one another in the street.

-Balance free time between finding a mate and

maintaining friendships. Men rarely ditch their buddies. Yet, sometimes women vanish on their girlfriends in a second when a man is around. Do not limit contact to using condescending pats on the head ("Girl, you'll find a man too!"). Be there in good times and bad. The bond will be strengthened and that woman will be more attractive in any type of relationship.

-Do not be a mule and take on the responsibilities of those who never reciprocate. In other words, the Sister should not have anyone else's back who does not have hers. We are not created to live a martyr's existence.

-Black women should place their own well-being first by not so much as sharing oxygen with a man who doesn't carry his weight.

-Black women should be especially prudent where they direct their dollars. Do not support music, TV, movies, and other entertainment that embodies a negative portrayal of Black women. If one listens to the garbage long enough, they will begin believing it. Fill the void with positive artists such as Jill Scott, Corrine Bailey, and KEM. I lean towards R&B, jazz, blues, and the oldies.

-A Black (or any) woman should make a pact with herself: No more shacking up, rolling in the hay with, financially supporting, performing "wifely" duties for any man without benefit of a commitment.

-Learn to trust a very important sense called "instinct." If a situation does not look, feel, or smell right, it probably should be avoided.

A Quick Note about Online Dating

Placing an ad online can be a fun and convenient way to meet new people. I encourage Black women to use this resource while expanding their options. Some people denigrate this avenue due to some bad apples simply wanting to "hook up." These damaged men can be found with initial flesh-and-blood meet-ups, so this is irrelevant and changes nothing. Many have found the love of their lives through online dating services. However, I do want to briefly address safety issues. Some may be common sense but we all get lulled into a false sense of security from time to time.

In the beginning:

-Meet in a public place. Stay in a public place.
-Use your own transportation initially until trust is established.
-Give a family member or close friend an itinerary. Timeframes are important too, especially when the date is projected to end. (No one is expecting a "to the minute" goodnight. By the way, first and second dates especially should not go on endlessly anyway. There should be a conclusion. Arrange to call that trusted contact within a certain interval; i.e., thirty minutes to an hour after 10 p.m.) If the

destination changes along the way, keep them abreast. Take note of the license plate number of your date, call that contact and relay that information along with the color/make of his vehicle. Yes, it's very romantic; however women are to be responsible for their safety. No harm in letting the man know you're doing this if there isn't an opportunity to be discreet about it. Your date's reaction will give an indication to his character.

-When going home, make sure you're not being followed. Better yet, stop off at a grocery store. Keep the 'ol eyes and ears opened!

Now for a less dangerous but nonetheless annoying occurrence of Internet dating timewasters. These men for whatever reason just like to go online and shoot the bull forever. We don't have time for that. Men know what they need to do in order to meet and eventually be with a woman. If not, he's probably a damaged man and who wants him? Timewasters can be difficult for the novice to spot. Timewasters can make the woman feel as if she "didn't provide enough information" on her profile, asking endless questions.

The Ladies' End of the Bargain

Let's make sure we put up a clear flattering picture, fill out the physical descriptors accurately, and answer the basics/general interest's questions in the profile. Detail overload is not necessary at this point. That is what the dates are for. Any time the woman feels she is on a pre-job interview upon initial contact, on the other end is more than likely a timewaster.

Traits of the Timewaster:

-Asks for more photos. (He wants a full body shot, pictures of the dog, and all your dead relatives.)

-He has no photo, or makes excuses about not having one ready to send...Next! If the gentleman has signed up for a dating service, this is more than a reasonable expectation. With near certainty, a woman placing an ad sans a photo will be looked over in most instances. Briefly touching on this subject, I believe that *some* dating services use shills without photos to hook women to keep them paying for the service. Because after a while they just *poof*, and enter in another shill. Not only that, who is going to pay $25-plus a month for a dating service and not post a photo? They cannot all be high profile! In addition, the one who I believe are using shills are widely promoted on TV. Looks can be deceiving!

-Asks endless/intrusive questions about physical description and other trivial matters. If the woman has taken a clear picture and described her appearance in the ad, then this line of questioning is unnecessary.

-Sends winks/smiles/flirts without much follow

up. Nothing quite gets off the ground. These back and forth messages on the service should progress with the exchanging of e-mail addresses/phone numbers.

-Long distance men (Living more than fifty miles away). Not to say that love cannot happen here, but there are plenty of men who make it a point to leave the eyes and ears of their community for nefarious reasons. Other men simply want a "phone babysitter"—again, we don't have time for that. As things progress, get more information, do not give money, and consider hiring a P.I. *(This is your life!)*

-Emails without direction. A phone number should be obtained in my opinion within three days. A date should be planned shortly thereafter. It doesn't matter too much *when* you guys can go out. However, the date should be marked on the calendar soon after a phone relationship begins. Also, do not hang on the phone forever waiting for him to make a date. Contrary to popular belief, men know what to do.

Contrary to years of programming these actions are not "acting White." It is called personal development. When a Black woman begins to hear this type of nonsense, she will know that those parties are trying to limit her.

Critical Thinking:

It is no secret that Black women have incredible

spending power. Between clothing, hair, home décor, and entertainment we keep our retailers in business. Black women are some of the most stylish, put-together beings on this earth. Even during times of lack, we have the uncanny ability to stretch fifteen cents into a dollar and still come out looking fabulous. Black women should *always* be careful to support avenues where they are respected, and is geared towards their interests. With that being said, everything advertised as "Black owned/run" isn't necessarily the best investment. Some entities take advantage of our buying power without regards to our well-being. Everyone who smiles in your face is not a friend! Black women should not direct their dollars towards institutions which endorse (actively or passively) calling her b!tches, h0's and everything else but a child of God. Whether it's degrading music, TV/movies, or even magazines which recycle the same bad relationship advice, this is extremely detrimental to the spirit over time.

Are Black women also hanging onto costly habits which no longer suit us? Our hair care routines often take up too much time and resources. I've witnessed Black women in the beauty shop three to four hours every other Saturday spending somewhere around $50 a pop for touch-ups alone. Not to mention the products, curling/flat irons. One must also consider the time it takes getting ready for work, home maintenance, and planning activities around hair. By reducing or eliminating this expense, a Black woman can easily have an extra

$150 or more monthly to save towards her interests. Another benefit will be the time saved. There are many wonderful natural hair care sites available. My blogroll has quite a few.

Black women say...

"Are we courageous enough to face facts regarding the unavailability of Black men to date and marry? Are we courageous enough to not care what others think or will say if we decide to date and marry outside of our race?"

"As Black women, we don't have to live a lonely life. We don't have to settle for men who are not as ambitious or accomplished as we are. We don't have to settle for raising children on our own because their fathers shirk responsibility. We don't have to settle for shacking up instead of marriage. We don't have to settle for men who are too proud to express affection towards us in public. We don't have to settle for men who are too dense to understand the value of emotional and financial partnership. We don't have to settle for men who are unwilling to provide for their families. Do not settle for dramatically increasing exposure to diseases, including HIV. Avoid the subgroup of men who value only promiscuity from women. We don't have to settle for men who have never grasped the concept that in most cultures, the ultimate proof of your manhood lies in how well you take care of your family."

"I would like to say that any man worth his salt is neither turned off nor intimidated by a high achieving, positive Black woman. In fact, those qualities only add to her beauty and make her that much more attractive as wives and partners."

"CW, I just watched your video and have to say that you are a beautiful, strong, Black woman and you make me proud to be a Black woman. I am so proud of Black women like yourself. It gives me pride every day just to know that there are Black women taking the steps to tell others that they MUST exercise their options. I wish that you could be featured in Ebony, Essence, or even be on Oprah where you can reach more Black women. I will be letting every girlfriend I know about these blogs. I hope that I will be able to see more of your articles. You are helping to liberate a lot of women. This is going to be the beginning of something new for me for sure."

There have been many positive experiences since expanding my options that I will be sharing in the near future. My outlook has greatly improved in the past twelve months. As they say, "The proof is in the pudding." Be on the lookout for more and visit "Black Women Deserve Better." Remember, God gave Hebrews the promised land, but they still had to get up and go there.

Visit Black Woman Deserve Better online at http://www.thecwexperience.wordpress.com.

There is a time when the operation of the ma-

chine becomes so odious, makes you so sick at heart, that you can't take part; you can't even passively take part, and you've got to put your bodies upon the gears and upon the wheels, upon the levers, upon all the apparatus, and you've got to make it stop. And you've got to indicate to the people who run it, to the people who own it, that unless you're free, the machine will be prevented from working at all!

—Mario Savio, Sproul Hall Steps, December 2, 1964

REFERENCES

Protect Your Fertility, *online at
www.protectyourfertility.org*
Lyrics
http://www.metrolyrics.com
Gucci Mane - "Freaky Girl"
Chris Brown, T Pain - "Kiss, Kiss"
Souljah Boy - "Crank Dat"
Lil Wayne Interview
*http://www.mediatakeout.com/20303/lil_wayne_
if_you_diss_me_ill_murder_your_children.html*
Shabazz, Attallah – As Told to Alex Haley
"The Autobiography of Malcolm X." Ballantine
Books, New York, 1965.

Blue Letter Bible. Dictionary and Word Search
for "fruitful multiply" in the KJV. Online at
cf.blb.org.

Blue Letter Bible. Dictionary and Word Search
for "wife" in the KJV. Online at cf.blb.org.

Blue Letter Bible. Dictionary and Word Search
for "man leave mother father" in the KJV. Online at
cf.blb.org.

Mario Savio Speech, "The Machine," from
en.wikipedia.org. *Text reprinted here is available under
the terms of the GNU Free Documentation License.*

RECOMMENDED READING

Jr, Pearl. "Black Women Need Love Too." 2006

Newbeck, Phyl. "Virginia Hasn't Always Been for Lovers: Interracial Marriage Bans and the Case of Richard and Mildred Loving." 2005.

Maken, Debbie. "Getting Serious about Getting Married." 2006.

RECOMMENDED BLOGGING

The following blogs are not all exclusive to interracial dating. They do not necessarily endorse this writing, nor are they affiliated with my viewpoint or with one another. However, they contain valuable resources demonstrating how Black women can live the fullest, most satisfying life possible. These sites set the standard for the non-stereotypical life for Sisters, for Black women (and their admirers) who unapologetically go after their dreams and get their hearts desire. Their actions do not subscribe to the Black Community Machine's programming.

"A Writer Dodging Bullets"
awriterdodgingbullets.com

"Acting White"
actingwhite.blogspot.com

"Angry Black Cat - Corrupt America"
abc.corruptamerica.com

"Aunt Jemima's Revenge"
auntjemimasrevenge.blogspot.com

"Beautiful Black Women, Happily Interracially Married!"
blackwomenwhomarrywhitemen.wordpress.com

"Beautiful, Also Are The Soul Of My Black Sisters"
kathmanduk2.wordpress.com

"Beauty In Baltimore"
beautyinbaltimore.blogspot.com

"Black"
interracialdating247.wordpress.com

"Black female interracial marriage E-Zine"
bfinterracialmarriage.blogspot.com

"Black Fire, White Fire"
blackfirewhitefire.blogspot.com

"Black Girls Like Us"
blackgirlslikeus.blogspot.com

"Black Girls Rule!"
blackgirlshaven.blogspot.com

"Black Women First"
bwfin2008.blogspot.com

"Black Women In Europe"
blackwomenineurope.blogspot.com

BLACK WOMEN DESERVE BETTER

"Black Women Need Love Too"
blackwomenneedlovetoo.com

"Black Women's IR Circle"
dateawhiteguy.blogspot.com

"Blasian Exchanges"
blasianexchangesanovel.blogspot.com

"Boycott Black Men"
boycottblackmen.com

"Brown Sugar"
brownsugar28.blogspot.com

"Dear Black Man"
dearblackman.com

"Diary of an Anxious Black Woman"
diaryofananxiousblackwoman.blogspot.com

"Everything Wrong With Black America As I See It"
everythingwronginblackamerica.blogspot.com

"It Amazes Me"
curiositykilledthatcat.blogspot.com

"Join The Revolution"
revlynn.blogspot.com

"Just Another Angry Black Muslim Woman?"

azizaizmargari.wordpress.com

"Kudzumonamour"
kudzumonamour.blogspot.com

"Love Me Some White Boys"
lovemesomewhiteboys.blogspot.com

"Prosechild's Weblog"
prosechild.wordpress.com

"Sangraneth"
sangraneth.blogspot.com

"Sara's Blog, Interracial Love"
sarasbloginterraciallove.blogspot.com

"Single Sista"
singlesista.com

"SisterCentric"
sistercentric-sistercentric.blogspot.com

"What About Our Daughters?"
whataboutourdaughters.blogspot.com

"White Men Who Prefer Black Women"
whitemenforblackwomen.blogspot.com

"Why Black Women Are Angry"
whyblackwomenareangry.blogspot.com

BLACK WOMEN DESERVE BETTER

"Zabeth's Corner"
zabethblog.blogspot.com

CW On YouTube

"Black Women, Shut Down The Straw Man!"
"Black Women: The Exterminator Has Been Here "
"Adam, Where Art Thou???"
"Are Black Women Getting The Love They Deserve?"
"RE: Black Women Under Attack"

I'm always looking for blog contributors and participants for "Black Women Deserve Better."
In Search of:
-Black women who are in committed interracial relationships/dating interracially
-Men who are in a committed interracial relationship with a Black woman
-Black women who wish to date interracially
 This forum is designed to help those interested gain perspective on the issue, making an informed decision, and perhaps meet some new people. Visit the forum to learn more:
 http://thecwexperience.wordpress.com
BWDB on Myspace
http://myspace.com/blackwomendeservebetter.

CW

Breinigsville, PA USA
28 February 2011
256549BV00001B/1/P